T0208362

THE MOTIVATED LIFE

A Study on Goal-Setting, Well-Being And Achievement

Developing African American Male Adolescents

By: Shellie Sampson Jr.

iUniverse, Inc.
New York   Bloomington

The Motivated Life
A Study on Goal-Setting, Well-Being and Achievement

iUniverse books may be ordered through booksellers or by contacting:

iUniverse
1663 Liberty Drive
Bloomington, IN 47403
www.iuniverse.com
1-800-Authors (1-800-288-4677)

ISBN: 978-1-4502-2248-8 (sc)
ISBN: 978-1-4502-2247-1 (ebook)
ISBN: 978-1-4502-2896-1 (dj)

Printed in the United States of America

iUniverse rev. date: 5/11/2010

Preface
Raising the Level of
Personal Achievement

The Motivated Life pulls together integrated perspectives about awakening levels of potential and success. It is about adolescents and young adults in educational transition. This integrated perspective includes adolescence, personality, the social environment, the school environment, goal-setting, and incentives.

This book brings together the author's many years of interacting and working with those finding their way in the world. He served as an urban school headmaster and was involved in community programs with adolescents and young adults.

The information presented comes together as a composite picture of a social and educational journey of some urban male students. It is a story, in fact, of the step-by-step challenges of those who are reaching for success (in a fast track world).

The reader should not be overwhelmed by the diversity of information including an actual study of some urban students in a major U.S. city. The reader may feel free to examine parts in detail, or scan other parts for general content. People vary in their specific interests, but together an entire picture is presented here about developing a motivational life.

It is profitable to look into the life-world of others to see more clearly the one in which you live. A successful life includes critical observation, reflecting upon diverse ideas and making better decisions. *The Motivated Life* encourages all struggling persons to think, search, and create a new life for themselves. Society is filled with those who are coping with the means and conditions of success in their own context. Many persons are suffering from a devalued life of underachievement. Success is usually desired, planned and executed. The purpose of this book is to help provide strategic information to move the lives of those who need it most, to a more productive level.

Contents

CHAPTER 1
INTRODUCTION

Why the Urgency of the Motivated Life?

He is not so lost as he who has no dreams.

—Anonymous

Life is defined by a moving motivation. Motivation requires a perspective on life itself. Personal direction, stability, and positive self-esteem require a clear focus and on-going effort. Chosen goals and involvements are carefully pursued. They increase the quality of life for the seeker. Motivation is not a stop and go operation. It is not a project by project task. It is an ongoing pattern with plan and purpose. It is a momentum.

Many social and scientific explorations start out with a key focus in mind that eventually leads to a wider perspective. Many investigations that seek information about a particular subject start with certain focus groups, test groups or segments of a population. Some groups have greater challenges than others in certain categories. In the case of adolescents in general and African American adolescents in particular, motivation and goal-setting is a major area of concern. Motivation and goal-setting continue to be important subjects in society.

This book *The Motivated Life* resulted from a long term study of motivation and goal-setting over many years. This study originally centered around achievement motivation of adolescents and young

1

adults in a school setting. But, after a period of time I realized that motivation is as much about a whole life as it is about specific desires, educational pursuits and success. Motivational thought and principles go beyond study groups and careers. It encompasses the entire range of life from childhood to mature adulthood. It is difficult indeed to live a productive and meaningful life without ongoing energized tendencies that move the person toward a satisfying level of well-being and personal development.

Maintaining high levels of motivation in most companies and institutions is a high priority. For most people who live in this complex global society the need for organized, planned lives is critical. There are personal, employment concerns, bureaucracies and institutional policies to deal with. Those who interact with schools, places of work, or businesses cannot afford to engage others haphazardly. Even informal social gatherings may require some degree of reflection for those who "plan" to attend. The motivation to present the best display of ourselves and talents should prompt our preparation.

The purpose of *The Motivated Life* is to reinforce the felt importance and application of motivational and goal-setting principles. The significance of motivation is most critical in for learning and planning for the future. The book begins with insights gained from three main sources. First, the literature provides us with an overview of the characteristics of adolescents and young adults in transition. The literature provides particular insights about motivational, social, and educational concepts. This information includes key ideas in goal-setting, success, role of the family, the school, neighborhood, and the influences of urban life. The reason for this overview serves as a reminder that motivational tendencies emerge from many sources. Some of these sources are obvious. Some of them are not. Many factors work together. To create a kind of trajectory or directional push that helps to move us in one direction or another. We do not live in a void. The places we go, the people we meet, and the things we hear can affect what we will or will not do. In fact, personal and social meaning is an acquired "taste". That is we not only develop our thinking from a pool of collective sources, we interpret that information from our own vantage point in society. If we are somewhat satisfied with the conclusion of our experiences we feel a sense of well-being. If our reflections on life do not lead to some sense of balance and well-being we attempt to find ways and insights that add to our satisfaction and minimize our anxiety.

The second phase of the book deals with the study group of Afro-American adolescents in an urban setting. This also includes motivational perspectives of experienced guidance counselors and others. The way the study was carried out is outlined for readers who may want to know. The study utilized research definitions, concepts, and ways of viewing motivation. This information was in turn used to measure and assess the various dynamics of goal-setting and motivation that affected the motivational life of the students in the study. This information includes factors relating to self confidence, preparation, personal habits, and hindrances to motivational life. The reader may select a section of particular interest to review in more detail in the book. Each section presents insights about motivation in regards to putting a more complete picture together on the subject of *Motivated Life*.

The third part of *The Motivated Life* uses information from the literature, the study group and related concepts to discuss overall applications. This discussion is for a wider audience of readers engaged in on-going self help tendencies. This discussion moves from adolescents to adults living in a complex post modern world. In this world motivational tendencies for success, achievement, and well-being are extremely important. The post modern world can be illusive, very competitive and fast moving. Motivated persons must be flexible, alert, constantly learning new things and new ways of coping and achieving. A motivational program is proposed in the book to aid those who need to engage a structured program for realizing success.

The Goal-Setting Approach for a Better Life

The book begins with an overview of motivational study in the urban context. There is no lack of research and data to document the plight and problems of urban adolescents and adults. There has been a stream of continuous dramatic publicity about the social difficulties of African American males in particular. Problems and concerns like:

urban life, economic well-being, poor social adjustment, violence, school failure, incarceration, and hip-hop music (messages) are often highlighted in the popular media. One question has stood out in this context: Do African American urban youth and some adults really desire to live the motivated, achieving life?

Carolyn Tucker, a researcher and clinical psychologist specialized in behavioral medicine and minority achievement orientation. Tucker states that most of the issues concerning African American children can be summed up into two categories: behavioral problems and academic failure. Many adults are also challenged by poor social adjustment and a failure to master any particular field. Tucker attempts to bring some factors together in order to confront the one summary issue of social failure. However, included in these factors are the restrictive and at times the oppressive role of urban life. We all have a domain (life-world) in which we live. The social environment and the historical setting of the times do affect our motivational orientation and sense of well-being. Experiences as "the other" in the context of clashing value systems and worldviews affects how we process information. These experiences include stereotypic labeling, severe economic disadvantages, and the challenges of fair, affordable judicial representation when needed. Yet, there are many good examples of those who have achieved despite the social, political environment. These persons have transcended their circumstances because they lived the motivated life. At the same time, others were experiencing personal and academic failures. These persons often experience a lack of clarity about coping options and relevant goals.

This book will explore the possible use of strategic goal-setting actions as a means for the many who struggle in disproportionate numbers to survive and thrive. The challenge of setting goals involves internal and external factors. This includes the perceptions urban youth have of their social context and educational institutions. The problems urban male and female adolescents face are compounded by the demands of a globalized, increasingly technological society. Global citizens must be able to learn and compete on a world-class market level. Anyone who does not think about his or her future could be at a serious disadvantage.

A few glowing stars cannot overshadow the on-going plight of the many. As the world becomes more troubled and complex, the numbers of groups that are struggling are going to increase. Nurmi and Salmela-Aro maintain that persons who have a low level of experienced well-being tend to be more concerned with existential (immediate) interests and demands. This may tend to distract their attention and focus from planned goal-setting activities. These persons are instead occupied with raising their conditions of well-being. Factors like tight income, tense family and peer interactions may affect well-being and relationships. Those who have high feelings of well-being and low stress levels are freer to focus more upon achievement goals according to their age, maturity and social conditions.

If this is the case, the challenge will be to encourage the adolescent or young adult to move beyond the existential preoccupation of everyday life and focus on the motivated life beyond mainstream needs and concerns. Striving persons must think more about the solution than the pain of the problem. The individual must not become dysfunctional and unstable. People must move from needed reflection of the social-political context to planned performance. New innovative strategies can help to minimize effects of shock and despair.

Practical Rationale: Why Goal Setting

My basic premise is that motivation goal–setting activities when practical can and ought to be the organization principle that orders daily life. Random thinking and acting on a "as you go basis" limits the accomplishments and well-being of the person. There is little control if there is little thought about short and long term goals. Most people especially adolescents need to engage in a goal-oriented motivated life. Adolescents need to be purposeful and meaningful in their personal pursuits. Life is more than electronic games, music, clothes, and leisure.

In recent years a growing interest has been shown in goal setting. Leading researchers assert that goal setting in African American youth has been under-studied. Yet, goal-setting is necessary for making value choices in the wider social context. Goal setting opens a window to understanding human behavior. It is one way for a person to move from the present into the future; it is a way for people to organize their lives and thinking. Goals can move people beyond abstractions to concrete activities. Goals make it much easier to exercise efficacy (controlling effects) because actual action steps can be identified and monitored. Having goal images helps to free the individual from current stimuli and distractions. Goal-movement allows one to peer into the future. Even changes in apparent goals can occur with more ease when the process of goal setting is already in place.

For the student, goal setting offers the means and the opportunity to develop and strive towards a meaningful future. The student can exercise autonomy by setting and pursuing personal goals. The adult can readjust his or her life through the discipline of goal activities. The person who sets goals must utilize primary factors that make up a sense of self and future expectations. In other words, goal pursuit requires a "know they self" examination. The activity of setting goals involves individual movement towards an integrated self. This includes intrinsic (internal) and extrinsic (external) information to pull together various experiences for self-directed development. Goal setting provides social and personal reasons for students to engage in schoolwork and achievement behavior. Without goal-vision the lives of people diminish because there is no incentive to take their lives to another level.

African Americans have always valued education as a means of social mobility, but have not always translated this value into effort and patterns for success. Freeman, Gutman and Midgley argue that this is important. African American students who endorse extrinsic goals from the environment do so because they tend to be more adaptive to the socioeconomic realities they must face. Achievement goals, by themselves, cannot be correlated with the overall academic performance of some students because of other factors, such as social relevance, social behavior, and teacher response to diverse students.

Kaplan and Maehr maintain that recent helpful research in achievement goal theory should translate into the practice of facilitating the learning and motivation of under achieving students.

They further argue that social research concerns should include the need to support the upward social mobility of these students and not just emphasize student deficits. It is not research for research sake. School performance in all schools should reflect the proper and applied use of goal theory to develop the student as a valued person. Often the best insight is not always used to help the student. Higher teacher qualification is no substitute for personal regard towards each student. (Rogers)

Task-oriented goals help the student to concentrate on the assignment and not other people. This approach helps to avoid self-handicapping ego goals, which tend to put too much focus on student comparisons. Task-oriented goals center upon task-mastery and student competence not the level of other people. The tendency to over engage in gap comparisons that don't always include other relevant information demeans hidden talent and potential yet to be developed. Gap comparisons may obscure individual differences and be used to justify categorizing persons in a restricted track or domain.

Life achievement goals afford opportunities to interpret the environment and construct personal meaning. Sandra Graham reports that concepts of motivation include what is to be expected and the value of a goal if it is achieved. This implies that there are value judgments at work in determining what is desired as an ideal in the future. The motivated life pattern goes beyond dealing with a specific crisis in the present. The person is more concerned with their whole future. This future anticipates a better quality and rhythm of life. The person experiences better cohesion if they can connect thought and action.

The literature provides support for a study of goal-setting tendencies of striving adolescents and adults by demonstrating the following: First, more research needs to be done on goal setting as a significant element of the motivated life. Second, the motivation levels of urban male students in particular are far from optimal. Third, the research that has been done in the past about motivation was heavily race comparative. This may or may not be an important factor for some researchers. But this study focuses on the motivation of urban adolescents and adults as significant persons getting ready for their future. The study of goal setting and goal theory is practical in dealing with family management and collective planning for connected groups. For example, motivated parents must learn about health care, budgets and relevant school conferences. At the same time these parents must negotiate their own employment conditions, transportation arrangements, home operation needs, banking transactions, legal matters, local political concerns, and other personal concerns which must be managed. Each family related institution must be adequately addressed to stay ahead of potential problems that pop-up from time to time. A motivated life style of diligence and perseverance becomes necessary in handling the many affairs of every family. The motivation life is organized around keen awareness. In other words don't wait until a problem arises. Work to "get your house in order."

African American Male and Female Differences

In terms of family roles, religion, social services and educational participation, the development of the African American male and female has been considered as different even though there is some overlap. Scholars argue that the Black female has exhibited a greater sense of agency, self-direction while encountering oppressive gender structures for many years. Society's response to the African American female's facial and physical appearance inferred that these females often lack beauty according to mainstream standards. High-achieving Black females are more likely to accept mainstream values than high-achieving Black males. Cokley maintains that they are more likely to value school achievement as a means of enhancing their self-concept and respect. They live more motivated and meaningful lives.

Black women's lives are nested in a matrix of power inequalities with other opposing realities. These realities could include Black males. Sometimes Black males with problems may not be able to treat Black females with the greatest respect. Other factors may include general social-economic restraints and the risk that come with gender preference in society. Given the regional differences of African American female socialization practices, a study group of African American males was done separately. There are none-the-less overlapping factors among many groups, including male and females. The constellation (combination) of many factors still reinforces the need for a more ordered life of goal-setting management. Many groups share similar needs but the degree and level of various challenges makes a vital difference.

The Constellation Effect: Becoming Unique

There are those who would argue that all adolescents should provide "similar responses" to problems that encompass all of society. The argument would say, for example, that most adolescents: want to be successful, want to be respected, desire financial stability, a secure environment and a good education. Most adolescents likely want to have their working mothers at home more frequently. Likewise adolescents of all cultures may like hip-hop music as an option for their contemporary entertainment.

However, the great impact of diverse societal factors operating in an unjust context is not mirrored in the lives of all groups. Secondly, the total interactive impact of each factor upon the next factor within a set of factors often produces a chain of unique reactions and results. This is aside from the effect of individual personal factors impinging upon the lives of minority male adolescents and adults. The end result is that some groups need to engage in more creative approaches to living a motivated life if the challenges for them are greater than the "norm", whatever that is.

The combination of being "the other" in the mainstream society, being stigmatized and poor, having a lower life-expectancy rate and a mediocre education at best places restrictions on the nature of possible accomplishments in a timely way. Urban some male adolescents and adults are more likely to experience a stop-and-search occurrence in some places that would rarely be duplicated in other places. The mental and emotional toil of the experience of growing up under more pressures would not be the same for all adolescents in all places. There is also the possibility that they some adolescents may have the mental assurance of certain social connections in the community with which they identify. Cornell and Hartmann argue that in addition to the social restraints of labor markets and political power, marginalized groups suffer from the daily reinforcement of degrading stereotypes. Sometimes even among "successful" adults there are social messages that are sometimes present with a stunning force. Success doesn't make a person immune from social obstacles and public resistance. However, *The Motivated Life* does provide strong incentives and records for planning an effectively managed life.

Bakari Kitwana, who is an expert on hip-hop culture, states in his book *Why White Kids Love Hip-Hop,* that because of recent technology and the information age, hip-hop has become a crossover phenomenon. Hip-hop has created another reality which has affected mainstream culture. This means that hip-hop has its own character of inclusiveness and worldview that allows others to hear the voices of hip-hop and identify with common social predicaments. For example, Kitwana claims that millions of American youth are out of work, have dropped out of school, are receiving prescriptions for psychiatric drugs, and have suffered on the economic and political terrain of today's society. They see hip-hop's message as a spoken word and hip-hop's music as a temporary refuge from old ways of thinking and living. No group, whether it involves Whites, Blacks, Latinos, Asians, or Native Americans, accepts everything that hip-hop culture proclaims. Each group is selective in what it sees as relevant, self-serving, and useful. Each group has its own forms of uniqueness. Each group also experiences different degrees of social hardships over given periods of time. There is a human commonality in post modern society.

Hip-hop also has the added feature of looking "cool" and thinking independently. It allows one to become a participant in a new fantasy world. It is not a prerequisite that other groups immerse themselves in Black culture in order to relate to its meaning. But many young cross-over groups can come together to make a difference in policy-making or political election results.

Kitwana says that commentators want to reduce the hip-hop culture down to the level of antisocial, immoral and barbarous happenings. However, Black male respondents in this study said that hip-hop music was liked because it deals with social reality and the (surprised) economic success of noted personalities despite social conditions. These personalities were living the motivated life even within the world of hip hop. The study in this book expresses a similar conclusion to Kitwana. Hip-hop culture provides a voice of truth and expresses a critique of the social ills in a society that appears to be hypocritical and oppressive. But, hip-hop which originated in urban areas has more urgency and significance for Black youth who have suffered the most from racial politics and as undervalued members of society. There is a difference between adopting a cultural ideal and living through its absolute realism. But in between, there are motivating factors that inspire many adolescents in diverse cultures. Many youth and adults have moved into the pattern of a motivated life.

Taking a Closer Look at Goal-Setting in Adolescents

After several years of working with adolescents and adults it appeared to me (and others as well) that many of these persons were living without plan and purpose. In other words, they did not appear to have a sense of direction for their lives. Even if they did some unknown factors or obstacles hindered their ability to achieve. So a study was undertaken to gain more insight into the orientation of a group of urban adolescents. The goal was to see if any goals and aspirations were reflected in the overall make up of the person and his/her life style. Some scholars believe that once you get past the basics of life like food, clothing and shelter the rest of what humans do is motivated by culture, society and personal make up. This includes both males and females although male students appear to have more difficulties in society. In light of the many problems among males study group was made up of urban males. In terms of urban minority students there are many pressures and circumstances that transcend gender. Goal-setting is a particular concept that relates to many people who live in urban, global, and diverse societies.

There are four important reasons that justify examining adolescent and young adults:

- First, adolescence is a valuable time period. The adolescent is faced with many tasks to achieve. During this period a certain level of personal maturity and planning should occur. It is a time to face the facts of life.

- Second, the constellation (combination) of experiences of many male and female adolescents growing up in urban America is unique. These experiences should be examined in their own light. The constellation or combination of factors such as class, location, ethnicity, and gender define the uniqueness of urban adolescents.

- Third, the nature of the social environment or urban social structure is in fact restrictive. Restrictive does not mean impossible, it means be aware there are many obstacles ahead. The intricate nature of the social structure is very relevant to adolescent life and achievement. All adolescents must view the future and plan their lives in the context of the social structure that surrounds them. The adolescent must understand the rules and challenges of these structures in order to achieve. At the same time, adolescents and young adults should develop a perspective and ideology that is pro-social. The goal is to develop wider relationships and personal networks. The Motivational Life expands to become inclusive of diverse others. Negative attitudes are self-defeating and divisive (turn offs). Negotiating structures does not mean buying into all the social norms of the structures. However, life cannot be successful without engaging and evaluating the social order. Motivation seeks to move beyond restrictions.

- Finally, goal setting can become a tool for developing an intentional life for adolescents and adults. The urban developing male and female need to develop the autonomy (freedom to act) that will enable them to set goals and attain them. The challenge is part of overcoming past historical social conflicts and move on. Global society does not exist to affirm hurting people. You can hurt all by yourself or engage the world around you in an intelligent positive manner. You can think better when your emotions are under control.

The Context of Observation

All authentic research has a context and an historic background that relates to the purpose and strategy of the research. History in some sense helps to determine the role we may play. Phinney and Landin maintain that research dealing with ethnic minorities is best done as a "within-group" study in time and place. This research model is desirable because it focuses upon the actual characterization of the target group. It does not evaluate based on an implicitly better standard of another cultural group. This within-group approach helps to minimize the risk that a deficit model for research imposes upon the group. This can be done even if the problem is caused by social factors in a larger context. Research findings can be evaluated in this context once the studies are completed. Phinney and Landin claim, for example, that the ethnic extended family as a unique entity needs to be studied separately. In the past the ethnic family was studied as a group in comparison with other families in society. It became subject to stereotypes and prejudices. Phinney and Landin also argue that an ecological model of viewing all cultural groups in their natural settings (niches) gives a more accurate assessment of the uniqueness of any one group. In this motivation study, the unique perspectives of those in the study were examined in their specific urban context. However, in the process of the study many insights of the motivational life were uncovered. Many of these insights may impact upon the lives of others.

The Public Space

The structural and social environment (space) is where the meaning of life is perceived and lived out. "Structural" refers to the order, rules, and ideas of society; it includes socially prescribed roles and interactions. The personal or subjective self interacts with others in the public space. "Subjective" refers to personal adaptations, energy, and emotions involved in social interaction. Lemert and

Oxford state that this is the place where a sense of self maintenance, planned activities and recreation are played out. People must be motivated where they are. Many factors come together and contribute to the creation of the person as a social product. A picture of the person is drawn in a context. It is in the social-political environment where the motivated life evolves and reality is discovered. This reality includes a prevailing ideology or schemes, (good or bad) that gradually emerge. This is why street life can be detrimental if out of control. It informs the mind-set and helps to form the person who thinks and decides.

Social Structures help to determine how social support resources are going to be distributed. This support includes, but is not limited to, education, health, employment, social networks, recreational activities, contacts, public information, and power relationships. Available resources help frame levels of social competence, manipulation skills, and goal. Oxford points out that there are structured conditions that affect the psychological well-being of the individual. Adolescents need to develop in environments that do not undermine their desire or capacity to set goals and achieve. This may not happen! If supportive, responsive environments are not possible or present, the adolescent should still be encouraged to set goals. Setting goals is a means of moving beyond environmental restrictions.

Dawson reports that the way resources, rules, roles, and access to information networks are distributed in society, forces us to take social structures seriously. Dawson also argues that social structures affect public opinions and ideologies. These structures include media, judicial, educational, and business institutions. Residential segregation, neighborhood poverty, and institutional policies function to sustain ongoing minority resistance to dominant societal views. The minority community can become a "counter public" in its social perspectives. These perspectives can include levels of social pessimism and a sober analysis of race realities in America even during challenging times. Some people may see these views as corruptive because they may discourage participation in general society. Sometimes practical experiences can motivate people to achieve in public life. Some highly motivated individuals will occasionally defy the odds and rise up. They could become business executives or remarkable scholars like the chemist Percy Julian and President Barak Obama. Ideology is a way to order the world and face the global realities of social structure where each institution is in many ways like a government unto itself. They engage in firm policy-making, hold political views and operate as impersonal hierarchies. Complex environments can, however, facilitate mental development when they are seriously engaged. Circumstances can provoke people to think and perform on a higher level.

Dawson holds that the more active the person is in society the more he or she tends to develop distinctive clearer ideologies through experience and exchange. Those who are less involved do not have to confront the ideas and inequalities in society. African American contributions and ideology is hidden when it fails to reach the public sphere of debate and discussion. It may even escape the attention of some isolated youth who need to think. Under these conditions, the experience of ideological conflict is not readily felt. It becomes an abstract yet present reality. In other words, unless the ideas and plight of the marginalized group are publicly projected and discussed, the less the group will be taken seriously and engaged. The importance of the group is minimized because its concerns are not elevated or expanded to a wider circle. When some members of the public hear of certain group needs they immediately feel they are exaggerated or untrue altogether. Even legitimate research about these concerns can be overlooked or ignored.

In regards to location, the 2002 U.S. Census reports that 52 percent of African Americans live in the inner city. Over 70 percent of all Blacks live in urban metropolitan areas. It is in this context that many problems and social failures have been experienced, both open and disguised. Most of this history is a matter of public record. This is not our focus here.

Motivation related data in this study included government and city documents, open-ended, semi-structured interviews and school statistics. Interviews along with other data eventually become a part of a larger study. This approach can be very effective in dealing with a complex problem in a holistic manner.

Questions about Motivation

In the Grand tour question was and is: What are the factors that encourage or hinder adolescent motivation life? How do adolescents define success? Do they seek help in setting goals or learning about future options? Are they willing to make personal adjustments in order to attain their goals? Do they feel they have adequate justification and opportunities to achieve?

The investigation sought to ascertain if any goal-setting tendencies were related to any social and personal perceptions these youth may have had. The investigation also sought to find what school-related factors supported student goal setting. This study is socially oriented in that there is a social and experience context from which the youth have emerged. It is also practical in orientation, as findings can be applied to programs that help youth engage in goal setting and entry into a motivation life-style.

The Significance of the Person: Building a Motivated Life

The problems of urban, dwellers do not take place in a vacuum but in the context of the larger society. Complex and restrictive social structures have either helped create social problems or reinforce them. Historians have provided extensive evidence about the conditions of discrimination and inequality under which striving urban males and females as well have had to negotiate their status and well-being (Franklin & Moss). Society has often proven to be an obstruction to be overcome. It is not the purpose of this study to establish a cause-and-effect conclusion for the social conditions of the urban adolescents. However, it can be clearly argued that structural forms, social norms, legal policies, and discriminating practices have helped to place certain groups at a distinctive disadvantage. This does not mean that opportunities have not existed for various groups but that difficult social conditions have often frustrated the motivation and realistic thinking of some urban groups. Often some adolescents have had to depend upon the urban subculture for support (Anderson). This study sought to explore the possibilities that adolescents and adults may indeed become optimistic and not frustrated in their personal aspirations. This under-studied factor will be addressed during the study. Diverse social factors involving well-being (critical theory) will be examined upon completion of the examination of key aspects of motivation.

This study is about issues of personal agency, or the ability to act on behalf of one's self. The question of goal setting alone would not be that important if impacting social structures did not exist. The realities and dynamics of "the historical moment," does affect our willingness to endure hardships and achieve goals. This study examines the significance of adolescents growing up in urban America and the possible aspirations of youth who are a part of this context. Elements of the macro and micro life experiences of developing adolescents work together in informing how they cope, make choices, and set goals. These include factors from large social institutions to personal encounters, problems and relationships. The long-term goal is to encourage all challenged adolescents to join the "yes we can" group of persons who are willing to do something with their lives. I call this *"The Motivated Life"*.

It could be argued that there are other ways to encourage urban males and females to achieve beyond goal setting. The theoretical basis for this method is that the goal-setting process has been tested with significant results as argued by Sheldon and others. Goals that are set and attained lead to increased self-regulatory efficiency, increased psychosocial well-being, increased pro-social activity and self-esteem. Goal setting also leads to more thought-out, productive philosophies in the individual. Goal setting has been used to improve academic achievement, to better social and peer relationships, and to increase occupational attainment. Goal setting plays a major part in mood stability, increased self-awareness, self-acceptance, and personality development. In fact goal-setting when fully applied becomes transfoundational. That is goal-setting orientation can be used in many domains. It should be taken seriously by concerned educators and reformers for a better society.

CHAPTER 2
ADOLESCENTS FACING
ENVIRONMENTAL COPING

Introduction

One purpose of this chapter is to provide background information about the coping lives all adolescents must face. Afterward I want to review challenges in regards to African American adolescents. This overview provides a historical and social perspective of urban adolescents. This background information helps to provide an understanding of the antecedent factors that help inform the motivational orientation status of adolescents. Next, the review provides current arguments or informed discussions regarding: adolescent socialization, urban coping struggles, time orientation, and school performance. All of these factors affect the motivation life of adolescents and young adults. The chapter concludes with a review on school counseling. The review also points out any apparent gaps in the literature. The review also serves to indicate a follow up study if one is desired.

Tasks of Adolescence

Offer, Ostrov, and Howard reason that the adolescent has several well-defined tasks that lie before him or her. These tasks focus on developing parts of the self, which include:

- The psychological self that deals with a maturing cognitive thinking system. While viewing the world. Leary and Kowalski argue that adolescence is the most anxiety-ridden period for many people.

- A social self that can relate to generalized others well

- A sexual self that can act with sexual responsibility

- A family self that can blend into a cohesive bonding unit

- A coping self that is able to handle personal problems, stress, and conflicts

- An achieving self (Schaffer) that is grounded in adequate preparation

- Multiple selves in response to society's demand for multiple selves associated with different social roles in context (Harter). Adolescents must deal with a multifaceted world. The adolescent needs to become flexible and relational.

The Self-Concept

Arnett maintains that one of the greatest contributors to an adolescent's overall well-being comes from his or her sense of worth or self-esteem. This self-concept is based on self-image, self-perception, and a sense of social identity. Arnett asserts that adolescents are always reacting to an imaginary audience. They are very judgmental and self-conscious about the judgment of others. The total profile for adolescent self-esteem or global self-worth includes feelings of academic competence, social acceptance, athletic abilities, physical appearance, romantic appeal, friendships, and creative behavior.

Adolescents and Social Views

"Social views" in this study refers to the combination of ideas, experiences, perceptions, and attitudes that inform individual perspectives that make sense about society. Most books on adolescents deal with such topics as identity, self-esteem, relationships, physical and cognitive development, education, and personal problems. There is little emphasis on adolescent social, political, and economic views. There is not much focus on the social and political persuasions, issues, and any power relationships that inform the motivational tendencies of adolescents.

Youth form images and impressions about society, peers, and school, Fordham and Erikson, for example, say that the maturing adolescent develops an ideological structure in regards to the environment as a part of his or her ego or selfhood. The adolescent must simplify and organize personal experiences so that he or she can better interpret and act upon his or her perceptions. Without a view of the world, it would be difficult to make sense out of life and make satisfying decisions. It would be quite challenging to engage in a motivational pursuit without some perspective. An adolescent's behavior must make sense to him- or herself; therefore the adolescent develops a subtle internalized ideology or way of interpreting the world.

David Moshman holds that mature individuals become rational agents by creating patterns of thought. Ways of thinking, reasoning, and knowing are constructed by the individual through social and environmental interaction. Mature adolescents begin to formulate, discuss, and justify their own ideas. The way the adolescent views and interprets the world results from a sense of freedom the adolescent develops within his or her environment. A sense of freedom, significance, and respect helps to energize most urban adolescents. The adolescent interacts with his or her own peers in circles that facilitate free expression and the sharing of personal views. These views are taken seriously by their peers. Even adults want to be taken seriously by others. This turns out to be quite a challenge for some marginalized underrated persons.

In regard to urban life and culture, Tricia Rose reasons that hip-hop culture replicates and re-imagines the realities of the adolescents social experience. She says that hip-hop negotiates and appropriates new economic, technological, class, gender, and race conditions. Social forces have especially shaped urban music, speech, dance, display of style, and identity. Rose further states that the innovative combination of Afrodiasporic forms and traditions, rock 'n' roll, the blues and the spirituals has created a new kind of "control" over the plight of being poor, undervalued, and angry. Blacks have, in effect, created a means to act creatively in their crisis of being disregarded and depressed. Response to real life experience became a form of motivational life in the absence of other major support systems.

Life in the urban metropolis has consisted of social restructuring, imbalances of power, and marginal employment in the context of molding personal lives. These conditions were clearly seen, for example, in Detroit, Philadelphia, and the south Bronx where the local community experienced social struggles but also creative art forms. The Harlem Renassaince is one of the greatest cultural developments in American urban history. Artists were engaged in various forms of social liberation and self-definition making. Hip-hop artists in America, on the other hand, had a different set of ideas because of their more recent urban experiences. These included drug wars, prison, and political hypocrisy. The hip hop culture has become a global phenomenon originating out of the South Bronx. It was the new Silicon Valley of entertainment. Yet it was related to the music styles of west African culture. (Oliver and Leffet). Rose argues that rappers created their own oppositional ideology born out of their felt social position as "dogs." They call themselves Snoop Doggy Dogg, Tim Dog, and P-dog. Those artists who have grown up in urban areas were able to make fun of ideas about equal opportunity and racial equality. Rose also argues that they critique law enforcement, government, media, and unfair business practices through articulated cultural contestations. Here culture critiques culture.

Thompson contends that hip-hop artists entertain and enlighten by testifying truth through their lyrics. At the same time, however, their ability to produce social change is limited. Thompson further states that artists, including Snoop Dogg, P Diddy, and others, do not claim to be role models for dissatisfied youth, but conveyers of a relevant social message. They claim they are responding to the demands of their art.

Patricia Hill Collins maintains that many African American women participate in popular hip-hop culture. They bypass scholarly venues and traditional outlets as mediums for their thought. These

African American women are caught between nationalistic race loyalty, gender oppression, and feminist self-love. They must confront unacceptable tenets of both feminism and nationalism. Hill Collins says that feminist ideology becomes more personal as it becomes a political response to relevant feminist challenges. John Pittman states that some hip-hop authors are burdened with the struggle for recognition and freedom. Even "gangsta rap" is really a disguised exaggerated metaphor used to make a point. The point is that both urban males, females, and other groups may relate to hip-hop as a mutual expression of social and political experiences. However, the pursuit for a more complete system of a motivated life is still needed despite the rhetoric. The creation and expression of new forms of music and drama is in itself a genre within the motivated life.

Harrison, Wilson, Pine, Chan, and Buriel report that there is a social necessity for minority children to develop adaptive strategies that promotes survival and well-being in American culture. They must develop a set of beliefs that indicate a worldview, and socialization goals for survival. These goals should become a part of the larger vision of the Motivated Life. A set of beliefs should include a sense of: personal responsibility, self-management, competence, goal rewards and a transformed self. Harrison et al. say that adoptive strategies are complex because of the bicultural issues of values, identity, and customs that minorities experience. People must discover the critical social pathways to success. Minorities experience different conceptual and psychological processes, as well as different environmental factors. The environment "produces" the psychology through interaction with social reality.

Erikson the well-known identity psychologist contends that developed ideology has compelling power. It has the power to create meaningful participation in society. According to Erikson, there is no identity without an ideology. They are part of a whole. Banks states that ideology helps to determine the positionality of Black youth. This occurs when youth are affected by their social location, social status, and subjective feelings. Ideology is a strong systematic term. Youth "orientation" might be a better term for those who have yet to mature enough to develop a systematic formulation of their environment.

The Social Context: The Fatigue of Growing Up

As Wetherell claims, social context includes in its meaning a pervasive, inescapable, organized way of life in the environment. The environment contains ideologies, economies, language, culture, technologies, relationships, and power inequalities built up over time. It is complex and multilayered. The urban social context, family orientation, and the public school system are major influences upon the development all adolescents face. The social context of possible opportunities in the environment must be seen and seized. When there is a lack of encouragement and guidance opportunities are lost. Constant failure to achieve or gain confidence building experiences contributes to the fatigue of growing up. In other words, the adolescent must negotiate a multi-phasic indifferent environment from a limited resource base. Inadequate knowledge of mainstream expectations, institutions, and social codes can prove to have major disadvantages operating with inadequate communications and weak adoption skills can prove to be frustrating and exasperating. Psychological health and achievement can be adversely impacted by the socialization process children face (Parham, White, and Ajamu). The fatigue of growing up facing one obstacle after another will tend to erode progress towards the formation of a motivated life.

Living in the Urban Environment

In many aspects, urban life is restrictive by definition. Wirth contends that high-density living, competing heterogeneous groups, mixed-quality housing, technological systems, and social structures affect individual life patterns. Social attitudes and relationships, with a constellation of ideas and personalities, help perpetuate the challenges of urban life. Younger people tend to migrate to urban areas, where life tends to operate at a faster pace. There is more interaction but less personal communication. Urban life tends to weaken bonds of kinship, neighborhood cohesion, and social solidarity. The rearing of children becomes more challenging in urban areas. People live close together physically, but not necessarily emotionally (Gmelch & Zenner). In cities, there tends to be more noise and air pollutants, along with more general stressors. Urban life can create a more intense *"anxiety society"*.

Urban Trends Affecting the African American's Quality of Life

Kleniewski points out that in 1870 about 80 percent of American Blacks lived outside the city. The years of 1870 and 1920, according to Macionis and Parrillo were great migration years to the cities. Kleniewski reports that until recently there was not a predominance of Black neighborhoods; racially distinct neighborhoods did not appear until 1916 to 1930. This trend toward "Black Belts" started with the great migration of Blacks to northern cities. At the same time, there was a growing ideological, institutionalized belief that Blacks needed to be restricted in terms of living areas, employment, and education. Zoning regulations and restrictive covenants were common. Violation of these practices resulted in White riots, house bombings, and the setting of fires. Blacks lived in enclaves. They were contained. However, the act of participating in periods of great migration from the south to the north in anticipation of the better life represented a mass public display of the motivated life. These families went to work in factories during both the first and second world wars. The great Harlem Renaissance as I mentioned began around 1920 was teeming with motivated life and innovation long before the drug culture destroyed a great cultural awakening which defied all stereotypic notions. One major effect of the mass introduction and distribution of drugs was that it disrupted a stable flow of life and which suffocated the success of the motivated urban life style.

Goldfield et al. reason that migration resulted in social and geographical structural changes, which in turn have resulted in ethnic isolation and conflict. Residential segregation and the decline of economic resources in the inner cities also resulted in lower quality-of-life levels for urban Blacks. There was a decline in overall social commitment to cities after Blacks migrated to these urban areas, which resulted in "institutional decline". Major social institutions and government services became less available to African Americans. In fact, both class isolation and race isolation have accompanied neighborhood or geographical isolation in urban areas. Boger argues that Blacks, the underclass and poverty have become inseparable ideas. White flight and the upward redistribution of wealth were reflected in the number of African Americans in the lower-wealth percentile (Stoesz). In recent times a reversal of city populations trends has occurred. Gentrification has brought about neighborhood shifts as whites have returned to certain urban areas like Harlem and Washington, D.C.

Cuomo points out that the definition of urban also includes the development of ideological and behavioral characteristics that lead to certain patterns of cultural and social life. Kleniewski reports that, currently, the changing economy has led to polarized power and poorer cities, which now have been restructured into stratified areas according to class. These practices are tolerated or accepted by those who often see themselves as the institutional gatekeepers and policy-makers of society. This ongoing hegemony has become a part of urban reality. Kerbo maintains that oppressive structural factors in society have become entrenched in our society. These structures can play a major role in slowing the progress of motivated groups in society. Social mobility, for example, can be hindered by educational and economic inequalities. Nevertheless, some African Americans have made economic gains and created a quasi-Black middle class. But, during times of extreme economic decline and collapse even all of society suffers from bad economic practices, mass outsourcing of jobs and whole industries.

Kerbo also reports that often parents lack the social networks necessary to pass any progress they have made on to their children. These children have actually done worse than their parents. Kerbo reports that many middle-class sons have ended up in manual, unskilled blue-collar work or in no job at all. Further, Blacks who are listed as middle class are still living with major wage inequalities. Kerbo states that what is worst of all is that a continuing population of distressed lower-class persons are going to persist if this trend of inequality does not change. In hard times, even "established" African Americans suffer disproportionately especially during selective layoffs.

J. Wilson points out that there has been a steady rise in a "ghetto underclass." Blacks are over represented in this class. The nature of underclass environments (which feature poor school quality, joblessness, out-of-wedlock births, and poor or no health care) contribute to domestic problems. Major urban areas in America have been hard hit by the prevalence of youth gangs almost ignored by mainstream society. Much of the recent rises in youth gangs are attributed to urban isolation and male gender-role socialization, where aggressive behavior is viewed as a positive characteristic. Some members of the gang population end up as a part of the prison population (Shelden, Tracy, & Brown). The ongoing drug trade on urban streets also contributes to the prison population. Many "dropouts" and "push outs" end up in prison. About 30 percent of Black males under the age of forty have been in or connected to prison (Holzer & Offner).

Prothrow-Stith says that adolescents living around public housing projects self-reported a history of exposure to violence, depression, and family conflict. These adolescents have been raised in violent environments; many students carry firearms in and outside of school because of handgun availability. Other situational high-risk factors for adolescent violent behavior include exposure to drugs, family violence, media violence, peer pressure, community violence, and policing practices. At the same time, many neighborhoods have experienced decreases in recreational and after-school activities.

Social Isolation and the Motivated Life

Boger argues that isolated socialization in the urban context with economic limitations, including limited affordable housing, restricts the exposure of Black youth to a broad-based circle of resources, ideas, and knowledge.

Rosenbaum, Fishman, Brett, and Meaden maintain that the entire question of residential mobility interrelates with educational and employment opportunities. African Americans of low-income not only suffer from low income but from poor schools and low student achievement. They note that by the time a Black child reaches the age of 6 or 7, he or she has already absorbed enough of the localized subculture (attitudes, perspectives, values) to render him or her psychologically incapable of taking advantage of any future opportunities. Sometimes their motivational tendencies are "bent out of shape."

For example, in New York State in 1990, 37 out of 39 of the most troubled schools were located in Harlem, South Bronx, Jamaica, and Brooklyn, where Blacks were heavily populated. The state's worst hospitals were in the same areas, as were the most unsafe neighborhoods, highest drug trafficking, and highest unemployment rates (Wade). Basic school competency failures were also extremely high in these and other urban areas regardless of the student's intellectual levels. This means that these youth are affected by the macro structures of urban areas, including poor schools and a lack of job opportunities. Again, development occurs in a context.

The price of social isolation is social limitation or disinterest in participating in the larger society. The larger society is the one that the child will ultimately have to encounter. Another price of isolation is the lack of a variety of role models. Rosenbaum et al. reports that seeing other students actually achieve can have a positive influence on some non-achievers. They also claim that according to their research, when some Blacks get the opportunity to relocate to the suburbs, they end up in more isolated areas outside the city. Because of White resistance to the practice of integration, Blacks end up trading one disadvantaged area for another.

Test scores of suburban Blacks do not differ significantly from the test scores of urban Blacks when both groups live in isolated areas (Rosenbaum et al.) If the movers lived in areas where the standards were higher, they did better, if they did not drop out of school altogether. The dropout rate for students who move to suburbs can be significantly lower than for those who move to cities, if the environment is better.

The Adolescent as "The Other"

"The other" refers to difference in relation to mainstream society identity. Difference masks feelings, attitudes, and conceptions that define the separateness of groups and individuals. Grossberg argues that otherness also recognizes the existence of those who have a contrasting presence in their "place".

Growing up Black not only involves an isolated context of urban adolescent development, but isolated relationships as well. Allen states that ethnic identity carries with it the challenge of dealing with negative social identity. The dominant culture views African American youth negatively, with lower status value.

Adolescents who have an awareness of this status as the negative other value their peer group membership, including membership in gangs, as a means of significance and belonging. Allen argues that feelings of powerlessness and isolation among lower-income Blacks increase the need for attachment. Social acceptance is very important to African Americans because of the Black experience of discrimination and segregation. Very often high rank membership in any institution, organization or social function can become a major source for pride and guarded status. Some African Americans magnify their own sense of belonging to avoid dealing with the stigma of human degradation and difference.

Allen also argues that African Americans are a part of the American society, as well as of Black culture. This means that African Americans have a social consciousness that goes beyond Black group membership. The African American racial and self-belief system is a multidimensional construct; the construct includes cognitive schemata involving race, class, social position, personal self-esteem, and stereotypical images imposed by society. Awareness of these elements exists in various degrees in the Black consciousness and becomes part of the individual's social inner reality. As a result, the individual faces issues of social legitimacy, recognition, and respect. A lack of these elements plagues many African American youth and adults who will fight if they are disrespected. This is why some youth place high value upon status symbols like clothing, body adornments, money, and hairstyles (A. Wilson).

A. Wilson says that youth respond to the external violence of social and racial oppression by being violent with one another. Youth who already feel isolated and have low self-ideals become even more isolated by choice. Some males who feel they cannot measure up to the values of the dominant culture become oppositional in attitude and behavior. Wilson argues that self-alienation results from fear, anxiety, ignorance, and insecurity; it eventually turns into anger and violence. Self-alienation becomes a defense strategy to maintain some degree of order and control; it represents a state of social and personal crisis. The person feels all other routes to satisfy his or her self have been blocked. The individual resents being in the place or state in which he or she finds him- or herself.

A. Wilson also maintains that adolescent ideologies about manhood and masculinity are adaptations to oppressive social conditions. The African American male feels forced to assert himself in the face of negative cultural images. The Black male's attitude towards the Black woman, who becomes a target of abuse, is just another outlet for Black male social and personal frustration.

Urban Coping and the African American Family

J. Wilson says that the Black family has had to go through three periods or stages of racial stratification in its struggle for economic and social survival. The pre-Civil War period of antebellum slavery was a period of strict, structured racial stratification. It was a dehumanizing form of economic and social repression. Even for Blacks who were not slaves, life was dehumanizing and oppressive. The second stage included the period of Jim Crow, immediately following the Reconstruction Period (1865–1877). Stage one as the racial-caste period was followed by stage two, the class conflict and racial oppression period. This was a very harsh period, where former slaves barely existed, sharecropping and laboring as they could whenever opportunities appeared (Myrdal; Takaki). Myrdal accuses Blacks of this period of managing their money poorly. The fact is that Blacks had to be excellent managers of their meager resources in order to eat, live and survive. One must remember that Blacks had no bargaining power when they went to market their produce. They were often given less money and I.O.U.s that they had no power to redeem. But, during this same period Blacks founded colleges and schools with sparse resources.

The final period, J. Wilson offers, is the period of the post-industrial global-market stage. Up until this period the dominant White society used every overt effort, including unjust laws and policies, to restrict Black social mobility. Following the World War II era, issues of racial inequality began to give way to a period of class conflict and global competition. Again, however, Blacks were still generally a part of the lower-middle and low economic class levels. Black families still had to struggle to avoid being totally absorbed into the class of "the working poor." Even the gains made through what could be called the fourth period of the civil rights era, which succeeded the Jim Crow period and World War II. The industrial age transitioned into some social regression. This regression saw the decline of school progress, effective social-political leadership on a wide scale basis. There will always be some form of leadership. But the quality and dedication of a significant number of organized advocates for the legitimate concerns of social justice has waned in recent public life. The wider community has become more celebrity, ideological and publicity minded. The historic issues of affordable education, employment, housing, health care, high incarceration rates and more recently drug-gun traffic, effective political leadership and quality of life for the masses still requires major attention.

Miller maintains that African American families are still impacted by urban poverty, isolation, and the harsh conditions of violence, despair, and drug trafficking. In addition, Miller argues that society has set and imposed "ideological standards" upon a growing underclass that defines for them how they are to live. It implies moralistic standards of taste, social skills, and more. Black athletes and entertainers undergo extreme, minute examination, criticism and censor. Although all public persons are subject to public scrutiny, society blames the general Black community for absent fathers, local drug dealers, criminals, unwed mothers, and unprepared young Black males. There are, of course, many factors that contribute to these conditions. Black families are subtly charged with a failure to control these unacceptable social conditions. According to society, the Black family has broken down. Model families are main stream families, and model conditions are the conditions society advocates. However, Franklin and Moss strongly argue that there is family sharing in the care and responsibility of children; Black relatives do extend their limited resources to help their families survive under duress.

There needs to be more study about time and effort expended on maintaining family economics and survival. It becomes difficult to monitor children, school policies, and related political issues under overwhelming conditions. The freedom to attend local PTA meetings can become a parental luxury.

Neighborhood Control Ideas and Aspirations

Rankin and Quane state that the neighborhoods of African American youth affect their socialization process. Growing up in disadvantaged areas directly affects Black adolescent pro-social competency, norms, and behavior. Pro-social competency refers to the development of positive social attitudes, efficacy, and commitment to educational values. Rankin and Quane also maintain that these neighborhoods have a level of collective efficacy or community beliefs about effort and outcomes. Often the neighborhood as a whole holds negative beliefs about opportunities in society. Collective neighborhood conditions and beliefs can affect youth and their level of aspirations. Adolescents get involved with deviant behavior such as sex, drugs, and car stealing to feel a sense of independence, maturity, and accomplishment. There is also an assumption by some people that African Americans have a high level of control in regards to what happens where they live. This myth is fading as the dynamics of globalization increases.

The adolescent experiences transformation even if there are negative outcomes. Lightfoot asserts that youth act to create their own opportunities. Way maintains that in an urban area that is often problematic and dangerous, relationships become a premium for male adolescents. Minority adolescents need and seek trusting peer relationships in coping with the urban environment.

Even when neighborhood risk and environmental dangers are obvious, adolescents who identify with a localized way of life will still participate in life-threatening activities. Lightfoot points out that this type of risk taking is pathological. But this is a negative form of coping. Adolescence is a period of active exploration of various experiences. This activity reflects a way to expand the self through a type of motivated life.

Spencer, Cunningham, and Swandon report that Black adolescent male efforts at coping are exacerbated because of discrimination.

Social forces complicate the identity and self-image development of urban youth. Political, cultural, economic, and cultural forces work against adolescent school achievement and goal-setting activities. Black adolescents are keenly aware of the values and social standards of the dominant culture. It is in this bicultural and multicultural context that minority children must evaluate real opportunities for attaining goals. There are scattered numbers of youth who manage to "*succeed*" on some level. It does not mean that most of them are major achievers because they do better than most of their peers.

Schaffer holds that the adolescent must also develop an "achievement self." It is the purpose of socialization to urge children to pursue significant goals and master the challenge of schooling. The person must live the motivated life – a pattern of personal pursuit. This purpose is reinforced by both the family and the school. Those students who have high achievement values and aspirations tend to perform better in school. However, other motives can interfere with the achievement motive and cause student failure. For example, the student may look for success outside of the school system; the student may value his or her relationships with others more than achieving in school; or poor grades and grade-level placement may cause the student to shift interest and commitment to other things.

Arnett contends that some African American students still have a problem with achievement efforts being defined as acting White. This is especially true if the adolescent's household has a low educational background or if the student population is majority Black (Farkas, Lleras, & Maczuga). The Black-White student ratio effect is still a question. Inferior local education also helps to diminish the importance of education in general, and promotes alienation and disinterest in students attending those schools. Downey and Ainsworth-Darnell argue that even though Black youth have been constantly reported as being overly optimistic despite their circumstances, some youth do set and follow through on goals. There is still, however, a weak correlation between attitude and behavior. There is also a difference between optimism and performance.

According to Muuss, youth who are experiencing identity diffusion and behavioral indecision tend to have weak ideological commitments. These youth have not worked through a personal system of identity or personal values. Otherwise acting like anyone would not be an issue. These adolescents are not in a position to critique, criticize, challenge, disagree, or question outside or social influences. These persons are usually inconsistent in their opinions and behavior. They have no permanent or firm commitments. They usually live a life in limbo.

A. Wilson reasons that goal setting for Black youth is like engaging in "dreams without means." The needs of Black youth complicate goal-setting tendencies because of the many unresolved issues at hand. Blacks have become commentaries of needs, wants, and desires, as consumers, but not producers. Wilson argues that Blacks engage in illusions of "somebodiness" without the sociopolitical power and organization of ownership. Blacks usually have very little production resources.

However, if there is some truth in these statements no one is completely void of resources. The motivated life involves a vision and courage to be. Youth can chose to focus upon a goal for success or a rationale for failure.

Youth and Time Orientation

Jones reports that goal-setting tendencies flow out of a temporal perspective. This temporal perspective is in turn affected by social and cultural differences. It is also affected by power relationships in society. People in society must believe that the future holds a reasonable promise for efforts leading to achievement. In fact, Jones argues that it is risky to have a strong belief in the future if there are no assurances in the present of rewarded efforts. Institutional bias has severed the connection between hard academic effort in the present and equal opportunity in the future. Reality hits you hard when you are in the streets most of the time. Again, this argument gives in to apparent existential (real life) hardship and eliminates a positive view for the future. The challenge of an undesired state should motivate the person to move towards a more desired state for the future. the climb from the bottom can be exerting. Chosen destiny and goal-setting is an appointment with achievement and success. If you can believe and proceed you will at least elevate your level of life.

Jones argues that Black youth generally prefer proximal goals rather than distal goals because they cannot rely upon future rewards in a restrictive society. But in America, distal goals are generally preferred for long-term planning and accomplishments. Global society in general is geared to maintain a long-range time perspective and calculated projections. Those that do not think ahead cannot move ahead. This takes training, discipline, and encouragement.

Jones argues that from a position of disadvantage, thinking about a rewarding long-term future may not be practical. Jones observes, reaching for a dream can be desirable, but under given circumstances the dream can be subverted. This is, however, a part of life. Dreams can give meaning to the present if they are put to good use, organized, and reinforced. But, without effort, you can dream your life away. Life can be nothing but a dream. Yet, the promise of a motivated life style can out distance the emptiness of an uninspired life.

There is a major gap in the literature on Black adolescent time perspectives. Jones is one of the few researchers who have dealt with the problem at all. I would argue that goal-setting tendencies are very relevant to the individual's time and social perspectives. The person must envision the future and the reasonable time steps it will take to attain an anticipated goal. There is some truth about marginalized people wanting immediate gratification. Why wouldn't they? Black youth need to know the difference and benefits of short-term and long-term goals. Proximal and distal goal setting occurs in sub-steps, requiring a disciplined use of time and planning. First, however, the adolescent must come to terms with the world beyond the teen's subculture and isolated worldview.

Youth and School Performance

Tucker says that there has been much reporting on "academic failure" among Black youth. Tucker also states that this term often is not defined or is ill-defined. The term does not tell us whether the child is capable of performing, or is not performing for a given reason. The term could be dealing with test outcomes or student effort, or could apply to problematic low-income youth or middle-class youth.

Susser claims that African American students have suffered from urban schools that do not meet the criteria of knowledge for the international job market in a technical society. There are conditions (for example, in the urban Northeast) of educational discrimination or benign neglect by class and race that have put Black males at a major disadvantage (while many amuse themselves). In addition the standards by which they measure themselves or by which the school system measures may be false, misleading, or irrelevant. The student may not even know what his or her grade actually means in the larger context.

As the poor-performing student moves into adolescence, he or she will commit him- or herself to deviant peers. Children who do not experience a sense of "fit" will involve themselves in nonacademic activities and tasks. These students become less motivated because they have become deficient in normal academic skills. They have failed to master classroom discipline, attention, and homework assignments.

Henderson and Dweck maintain that motivation and school performance involve more than drive or motive. They involve the total psychological process of the adolescent. School motivation differs from general individual motivation in that the school provides the organizing structural framework through which the student must negotiate (Jarvela & Markku). The student must be able to adapt to school conditions in order to achieve. Maladaptation leads to debilitating patterns and failure; students can disengage from studies and undergo withdrawal. These authors point out that the ideas and beliefs students hold affect their motivation, goal-setting tendencies, and performance. These beliefs help to determine whether or not the student is willing or able to adapt to school challenges. Kaplan and Maehr argue that schools do not hold the same amount of power over African Americans as they do over Euro-American students who feel they are a part of the mainstream. Students who are unsure or ambivalent about their relationship to the school or fail to adapt well are more sensitive to obstacles and negative feedback. These students are less likely to engage in problem-solving strategies for success. To them the school has no real or practical authority over them.

Schlenker and Weingold point out that goal achievement is dependent upon creating a particular kind of identity in a situation. The individual should be able to respond to a situation that exerts a particular kind of pressure to achieve a certain goal. Students who fail to respond to those who create the behavioral script will drop out. In other words, students need to learn to adjust to the rules. The school needs to as a school exert some kind of push to attending students. Motivation comes from the reflective self and interaction with positive pressure from social structures (Allen). More attention needs to be given to macro-structural factors that impact upon the specific social context of Blacks. Self-concept management is about the ability to organize several selves (family, peers, and school/academics) in a given context. It is not just about positive self assessment of the general self. Ogbu contents that parents who have become disillusioned about the job ceiling for Blacks have allowed their feelings to have an adverse effect on the academic behavior of their children. Black children have a difficult time taking their schoolwork seriously and being perseverant. Ogbu argues that interviews with Black parents indicate that they were sending mixed messages about hard work and the "system." Parental attitudes about the social system are important.

Goal-Setting and Counseling in Urban Areas

White and Cones report that Black families have suffered from social, economic, and emotional hardships. Black teens in particular experience intense conflicts among their school peers. They need counseling intervention by school professionals. This would include career planning and goal setting. Sometimes the separation of school and adolescents occurs too early in the teen stage, before healthy attachments have helped develop them into more mature personalities. These youth are subject to feelings of anger and shame because of contextual social conditions; they often develop negative personal ideologies and related maladaptive behavior. Even though the Black family may value education, Black youth may be subjected to other cultural feelings and influence if proper counseling does not occur.

This does not mean that indifferent, mechanical, counseling will be effective if he individual student is not a serious object of concern.

Goal setting is hindered in African American males because of perceived social realities. Adolescence and early adulthood is the stage that is very judgmental. African American youth tend to have high aspirations and lower expectations. They often believe that structural factors, like school and social difficulties, and cultural issues will work against them. In addition, White and Cones maintain that Black male vocational perspectives are often limited because of overt and covert barriers in society. Resources required for adequate Black adolescent counseling may not exist in many urban school districts. Therefore, White and Cones insist that mentors are needed.

Letendre claims that in the United States adolescents are considered mature when they are able to act like adults. Autonomy is to have the ability to be adultlike without further help from adults. In Japan, teachers organize an elaborate system of guidance and motivation as a part of their mission. In contrast, in the United States, the teacher's role is seen as promoting an independent sense of self in students, so that the student will take on the responsibility for personal achievement. An elaborate system of guidance is not seen as necessary. I would argue that guidance may be less necessary with orderly middle-class students, but for students who have a problematic background, an elaborate system of guidance may be a necessary part of the educational process. A functioning relevant guidance system helps to indicate how serious the school is in helping the students as opposed to a "get it if you can" approach. This study includes feedback by students concerning guidance.

McClelland says that support networks of help, information, and opportunity can be incorporated with the thought and actions of the goal setter if a positive assessment about opportunities is made. Individuals will tend to change their ways of thinking and acting if goal opportunities are present. Ongoing goal-setting actions become likely only if the person perceives life-improvement results. The person must integrate goals into his or her system of daily life. In other words, McClelland argues that goals cannot be sustained if they exist outside of the person's normal thinking and behavioral patterns. Goals must become a part of the defining self. I agree with

McClelland that goals must be internally integrated with the self, but with the help of counselors. A good guidance system can, over time, help the student incorporate positive thinking about opportunities through reflection and goal setting. Then the motivated life can be pursued.

McClelland points out that the impulse to act must be accompanied by the opportunities to act in the environment. The environment must respond to the motivated person, who interprets this response as a signal to proceed or withdraw. McClelland, in a classic analysis of motive acquisition, argues that persons who have advanced reasons to believe that they are justified in having a motive or goal will respond better to educational attempts to help them develop that goal. Counseling efforts can have greater results as well. Individuals need to feel they can and should develop a goal. McClelland also contends that people need to perceive that realistic assessments of reality and available networks will work in favor of the individual's pursuit of a particular goal. Counseling would make this clear to the adolescent.

Summary

The central findings of this part of theory and literature review emphasizes three aspects of male adolescent urban life. The first aspect involves the period of adolescence as a stage of coping and adjusting to social and personal challenges. It is a period of coming to grips with the realities of the world and the ability of the adolescent to adequately manage conflicts and roles and the development of their physical, social, and adolescent selves.

Secondly, the review addresses the problems of growing up in a restrictive environment. The Black adolescent in particular is a member of a long-term marginalized community. The problem of lack of affordable housing, under performing schools, and inadequate fair employment has existed for an extended period of time. This experience in turn adds to the fatigue of growing up. That is, there are so many challenges present in the urban environment of adolescents that a succession of challenging episodes impacts upon their behavior and well-being. How the adolescent comes to view school, society, and preparation for a future is a result of his or her socialization process in the urban context. Elements of this stage affect the routine adolescent life, academic striving, and daily preoccupations with the demands of a complex society. This is a society filled with inequalities and one-sided power relations. There is no need to be shocked now.

Thirdly, the adolescent must deal with his social identity as "the other." Structural sources of turbulence, anxiety, and labeling confront the adolescents as a group. Alternative involvements such as hip-hop culture, dressing styles, mannerism, leisure, and attitudes can affect how the adolescent wishes to pursue future interest. The literature strongly supports the notion that Black adolescents tend to live their lives as a counter public. This state of affairs can hinder the need to participate in the knowledge of mainstream society and how it functions. It is a matter of focus not uniqueness and pain.

All of these factors discussed in the literature impact upon the motivation and goal-setting tendencies of Black urban males. I shall discuss how goal-setting dynamics relate to adolescent understanding and performance according to research in the literature and mystery. The main objective of course is to prepare the willing individual to move towards a more holistic motivational life.

CHAPTER 3
THE DYNAMICS OF GOAL-SETTING MOTIVATION

Introduction

This portion of the motivation review examines some major findings on the dynamics of goal setting and motivation. Questions used in the study to interview adolescents are based upon goal-setting concepts. Goal setting is a process that occurs in a social context, therefore an understanding of motivation and goal setting must reflect the context. There are unique motivational elements that may be strong in one group and weak in another. This is a study about a particular group of urban adolescents situated in a particular urban context. This review is also about shared concepts about motivation that affects many groups in diverse places. Goal-setting itself transcends age.

This part of the review discusses the arguments of various researchers in the motivational field. The aim of this review is to develop a comprehensive overview of goal setting that will help formulate a more holistic and contextual model of goal theory for dealing with striving adolescents and adults. Adolescence is the bridge to adulthood. There are challenges and issues regarding the relevancy of certain concepts and studies done with different groups of adolescents. The question of relevance in a few key motivational theories was explored. Adolescence has its similarities and its differences in regards to the motivated life.

General Theories

Personality and Choice Behavior

There are different approaches to theories about motivation. One definition of motivation according to Weiner is that it is a form of choice behavior. Choice behavior involves intensity, persistence, emotions, locus of control (in the person), expectations, and levels of aspiration. This is a cognitive (thinking) view of motivation. I would argue, however, for a broadening of this view. Adolescents think and make choices in line with their sense of self and experiences in the environment. Goal expectancy comes from past experience. Accumulated experiences also affect personal levels of aspirations. Past experience can also inform present attitudes, personal perceptions of ability, needed effort, and assessment of task difficulty. This is an attribution (cause and effect) process. The individual selects the rationale for the prediction of outcomes. The individual anticipates that his or her actions will have specific results. This may or may not be accurate or realistic.

Beck point out that personality determines motivation. People have certain natural tendencies to act. If a person needs to have power, he or she will then set goals to help him- or herself attain that power perhaps through a position of authority. General goals consists of personal items like enjoyment, self-asserting esteem (positive presentation) and interpersonal affection. Avoidance of the negative or anxiety reduction is also a goal in reverse. According to Mook, once goals are imagined, goal seeking breaks down into a series of approaches. These are called approach responses. The imagined goal stimulates or motivates us to do something. Whatever we do about the goal becomes a series of goal-steps (goal hierarchy). Caprara and Cervone maintain that the affective or emotional state of the individual influences the motivational state. The affective state influences the cognitive process by which the individual regulates his or her behavior.

When goals are present, they likewise influence what information is sought and assessed. Goals reflect a weighing out of standards and actions. Motivation involves standards for performance, effective self-education, self-efficacy (control) and setting goals. Standards are internal judgments about what is appropriate and praiseworthy; they are internal guides. People have a tendency not to act until they meet their own criteria for action. People must feel good about themselves through the standards they set. Goals represent the results of self-imposed standards for action. However, the person must have a learned sense of what is valuable and what is not.

The question becomes are adolescents able to set any standards? Self-efficacy (control) concerns what one is able to do must be in line with who the individual is and what is good for that person. Goals are mental representations of aims involving forethought. Goals must be accompanied by an interrelated system of standards, efficacy, and self-evaluation. This is called a goal-construct. A satisfying goal-construct sets the stage for personal action. However, a strong affective (emotional) state can override cognitive (rational) goal-constructs. That is, the person can experience emotions about something and act without formal reasoning. This is why feedback is needed to influence the persistence of authentic goal action. Some goal areas can be intimidating.

Ryan, Sheldon, Kasser, and Deci reason that questions about the goal-setting process should begin with "why": Why is the person pursuing the goal in the first place? Goals must have significance for the person and originate from the person. Ryan and others contend that goals which are the result of outside pressures, like the social environment, schools, parents and others, will have less impact than goals originating solely from the person.

There is a difference between imposed goals from parents or schools and autonomous goals that have resulted from personal reflection and conceptualization. Ryan also points out that another significant question about goals is: What factors have led to the setting of goals or to the lack of set goals? The person can exhibit personal autonomy by choosing not to choose. If this is the case, what is there about the environmental field that has failed to engage the person's motivational goal-setting process? Why has the person failed to participate in the motivated life style? Does the person feel a part of the real world? Or has the person withdrawn from seeking a more rewarding life in a particular setting? Everyone needs relevant sources of incentives, inspiration and engagement. These concerns have great relevance to marginalized populations who may be ignored in urban areas. Research addresses the impact of the environment upon the choice behavior of the adolescent.

Behavioral Versus Cognitive Goal Theory

Behavioralists define goal setting through behavioral (outward) outcomes. Persistence, active searching, and response to powerful incentives lead to goal activity. Behavioralists argue that the person's intentions are irrelevant. Real goal setting is observed through actual performance. If people are really motivated you will see something happening. The environment stimulates individuals to act. Conditions affect people. Irrelevant information will not cause the subject to act. Many people may have so-called goal intentions but have no response action to account for the specified "goal." But in contrast, cognitive thinking theory refers to the activity of the mind and how it is organized and motivates the person within a given culture. The focus is on mental not behavioral activity. This emphasis also reinforces the theory that motivation and goal setting make use of what is already known and exercised in the mind. It refers to goals as knowledge structures (Kruglanski). In this light some adolescents are restricted by their urban environments from having a wide range of provocated ideas. An environment void of positive stimulation and content limits what people have to work with. It has very little incentive power for persons to act and respond. The environment can affect the person in an unknown way.

Where I am Affects What I Do: Context and Goal Setting

Caprara and Cervone maintain that goal context is significant. If little information is provided by the social context, the person will be handicapped in carrying out any goal. Neither will the person be able to measure self-progress toward a goal for which there is little feedback. I argue that this is why mainstream social exposure or resources present in local schools and neighborhoods are an important

43

factor that need more study in regards to motivational incentives for urban adolescents. Schools should be, above all, motivating institutions. Schools by their very nature should be exciting, relevant, and persuasive. Goal setting theory must include factors that deal with the impact of incentives, conditioning and the stimulation power of the environment.

Goal conflict emerges when there are different demands and values from different sources compete with each other. If the motivating power of a particular source is weak it becomes virtually useless. This makes the questions about uniqueness and relevancy in the environment significant. Hickey and McCaslin state that the context can convey information that helps to encourage or discourage the sense-making process within the individual. This reasoning and relating process affects student goal orientation and energizes self-efficacy. The existence of a learning environment projects and personifies certain seductive tendencies and attitudes towards students. This environment should offer the best as it relates to its student clientele. This is why the nature of the school ethos is useful in ascertaining its "educational friendliness" towards all students. This information can provide additional perspectives on influencing goal setting develpment. It also can show the benefits for extrinsically (external) motivated actions. Predispositions and personal tendencies are helped and developed in the learning environment. This influences the "readiness to learn" orientation of the student.

Goals and motivation can be seen in a cultural perspective. Goals are a part of human agency, which is embedded in the contextual life of the individual cultural matters. Goal setting means the individual is willing to take action and do something for his- or herself in a setting that makes sense to the person. The social context helps to define, facilitate, constrain, and generate goals. In other words, Marcus, Kitayma and Heiman argue that goals become available to those who interact and participate in the collective life of society. Even goals that originate from personal memory reflect the stored environmental experiences and circumstances of the imagining person.

Goals the individual adopts or does not adopt reflect deeply held beliefs or concepts about the self. Goal setting reflects the state of the individual. Is the individual ready to learn more and do more and become more?

Goals and My Mind

Bandura maintains his opposition to the belief that goal setting begins in the incentive context. Rather, in his social learning theory, the thoughtful person is attracted to desirable goals in the environment. Bandura points out that goal setting is entirely cognitively organized. Cognitive (mental) organization is independent of the pull of an unrealized state. Bandura argues that the individual first engages in forethought, and forethought is translated into initiative and guides for intentional behavior or goal setting. Challenging goal incentives can enhance but not create motivation. Goal setting is an internal activity. Bandura argues that the individual must begin goal-setting actions by reflecting and setting personal standards of satisfaction (values). Self-evaluation consistency of competence, perceived self-efficacy (control), and the adjustment of personal standards must occur. The person is finally satisfied when personal standards are met. In other words, when a person reasons out justified effort, he or she might act. This helps the person to decide whether or not to engage the motivational life.

Bandura correctly recommends that people should cultivate reflection, intrinsic interest, and personal meaning before jumping into a task that does not matter. He argues that goal instruction promotes specific focus, technical skill, and self-initiated intrinsic interest. Students can be encouraged to develop their own standards and sub-goals. The student can in time develop meta-cognitive skills and be able to organize one's own thinking and reasoning operations. Meta-thinking is thinking about thinking. Bandura argues that individuals should not depend upon external rewards and incentives for benefits. This can be unproductive. Bandura says that if external environmental factors controlled human behavior then the actions of people would be completely unpredictable, depending upon changing contextual circumstances. Environment effects may not be that extreme but they are impacting. The objective is to be able to manage self objectives. Bandura claims that only those who have developed a self-regulatory capacity will be able to set goals and carry them out effectively and efficiently (without unnecessary strain). The student will be hit with fewer surprises if he or she does his or her own work in obtaining needed knowledge ahead of time. I would argue that all of this sounds good, but the practicalities of the environment can impact how and what the individual reflects upon. Few people, especially adolescents are immune to environmental, social, political and economic turbulence. This would be quite an accomplishment. Reflecting upon external realities is in itself a contextual consequence that diverts attention.

Bandura presents a very persuasive argument about goal setting and efficacy. Many of the factors he emphasizes should be impressed upon adolescents despite the limited role of the environment in his theory. The role of forethought is important. Thinking through a subject, having aspirations, and making personal adjustments towards desired goals are critical. If reflection is painful, trained counselors will be needed for therapeutic dialogue. Bandura maintains the importance of having aspirations, even if there are no immediate results that can be seen. Bandura also states that personal beliefs about competence and ability should not be a controlling factor that governs one's life and willingness to move on. People feel different ways at different stages in their lives. This is a relevant emphasis for struggling Black adolescents; learn how to move beyond painful criticism to a motivated life.

Bandura, however, does not answer the question of where goals originate. If a person has forethought, the images come from some source. Even if goal setting is entirely cognitively organized, the question becomes, how is cognition organized? Does the mind develop in a vacuum? Does language help organize cognition? Cantor and Fleeson reason that a person needs to develop social intelligence before he or she can mount an intelligent goal pursuit. This means that the environment must be understood and interpreted before real goal setting occurs. The press of the "life environment" is real. Also, Bandura ignores the role of power in relationships. He does not consider the reality that personal (self) efficacy is affected by the position and status of the individual in a relationship. He does, however, admit that the socio structural environment does impinge on people with or against their will. Different people are affected in different ways by the environment, depending on who they are. Bandura argues that in spite of the environment people tend to give up easily or think their individual effects are too inadequate to impact the environment. He says that people help make the environment what it is. People have always sought to control their environments according to Bandura. He maintains that if people relinquish too much power to authorities and institutions in the environment they cause them to become even more powerful. The use of available knowledge is affected by social structures, class, race, and contextual norms. According to Fleeson social structures mediate information flow to the public.

Oehingen and Gollwitzer state that many goal-setting distinctions come from behaviorist thinking. For example, the behaviorist emphasis on need gets translated into a need for achievement, a need for social approval as motive. Therefore, goal implementation has received more theoretical and empirical attention than goal setting as such. Even in regards to the environment, the concept of goal setting as applied action would begin only after social contextual cues became personal expectations. Cognitive activity, if any, does not operate fully until contextual effective conditioning has occurred. Matters such as self-evaluation, external concerns and rewards, and self-efficacy judgments are after-the-fact activities. People tend to reflect on eventful stimuli. The use of deterministic behavioral reasoning could still lead to an over emphasis on the social role of the conditioning environment. This could influence people to give up on personal effort to change their situation.

In contrast, cognitive view theories argue that personal volition (will) or motive, when present, will regulate behavior. There will be a goal-pursuit action that will follow the invisible motive. Specified effort will mediate a task or master a performance. The person will strive to do more or learn more. The individual will actively seek to attain an end state or satisfied the need for subjective well-being. The cognitive theorist cannot read the mind but in fact assumes that a mental application is going on, leading to energized striving. Goals operate in the personal service of autonomy or self-determined action within a given social environment.

Looking at goal setting from a contextual view means that there must be a social point of contact and border crossing for adolescents living in segregated neighborhoods and isolated cultures. In other words, something must be done in order to connect. Getting good grades and pleasing peers may cause conflict, but is necessary. Society can be cruel but rational thinking chooses to negotiate social reality. Parents, teachers, and students may have different or conflicting goals and values. But students must weigh the responsibility for striving for a meaningful life.

You Have a Path to Walk: The Goal-Setting Process

Carver and Scheier contend that no action can proceed towards anything until the final purpose of the intended act is known. This implies a thought process is occurring. The decision-making process involves two steps. First, the individual screens available options in the environment in light of some personal criteria (time, cost, availability). If it appears that there are not too many violations to the criteria or conditions set, then action can proceed to the next step. The next step is making a decision to pursue the considered goal. Carver and Scheier state that the two-step theory alters the usual goal-setting theory in that people don't project too far into the future. Decisions about what to do about a goal follow more immediate decisions concerning feasibility and ability. Every step in the process requires a decision. In addition, this theory seems to suggest that the individual looks first at the opportunities and hindrances already present in the environment before a firm commitment is made. I would argue that this is not necessarily the case. People can declare their interest in certain goals for many attractive reasons without attempting to examine the challenges and obstacles to those goals. Often strongly held values will move a person to go for the goal without a step by step analysis. Adolescents may not have the values, skill or experience thoughtfully to embrace a goal no matter how worthy the goal may be.

Bargh and Gollwitzer maintain that there is a link between environmental events and intentional behavior as a response. Goal-directed action can be stimulated by a set of features present in the environment. In fact, they argue, by having a repetition of environmental stimuli, individuals can in time respond to related stimuli. The problem is that some people will not be available for this kind of repetition. The social environment can affect goal setting by making it difficult to respond to certain stimuli. Mainstream persons who know best how the environment works can use the environment to further their own ends. In any case, the environment plays a critical role in whether or not a goal moves towards completion. Bargh and Gollwitzer state that there can be environmental "control" over goal setting. It is just a matter of what strategic route can be taken in order to exercise environmental mastery. In the case of Black adolescents, for example, if the sociopolitical system exercises control over the major institutions in society, youth must understand, prepare, and adjust to them in order to succeed.

The environment can set up obstacles to frustrate economic, mental, and educational well-being. Bargh and Gollwitzer report that the individual must be willing to make trial and error ventures as ways of thinking and succeeding. The individual must be ready to test environmental responsiveness. Would the environment open and respond if I engage in positive risk-taking behavior? Cantor and Fleeson argue that prolonged social constraints and personal delays act to produce anxiety and uncertainty. This discourages goal-setting behavior. The more a person thinks about a problem, the more possible challenges can begin to produce self-doubts.

In all goal pursuits, there is a risk of underperformance. This is called goal anxiety or discrepancy. Discrepancy is the conflict between will or won't. Goal discrepancy occurs when the person aspires to accomplish a task but intensive memories of past failures cause the person to reduce his or her goal level. Goal anxiety involves contradicting feelings of failure that work against goal aspirations. There is a discrepancy. Leary and Kowalski contend that environmental stress, personal anxieties and the opinions of others all affect the motivational life process and performance. The person worries too much about his or her ability to cope.

Achievement goals are related to the personal value system of the performer. Goals must be useful (utility value); they must be of interest (intrinsic value); they must be worth taking a risk (reward value). And they must be related to improving self-esteem (ego value). Goals must also be satisfying for personal problem-solving (solution value). The student should use realistic norms to accurately assess the reasons for success or failure. Some norms for measurement range from ability, study time, concentration effort and personal organization. Evaluation skills should be taught.

Useful Adolescent Goal Setting and Theory

Much of the research done in regards to motivation and goal-setting tendencies has had little relevance in understanding of the unique motivational tendencies of urban African American adolescents. Graham argues that much of the literature in the past has been concerned with highlighting Black adolescent failures in the light of other middle-class persons rather than helping Black adolescents to succeed.

Past research in motivation and goal setting has usually centered upon personality, attribution theory, self-esteem, behavior, locus of control, intrinsic-extrinsic motivation, drive theory, delay of gratification, need for achievement, competence, incentives, and cognition. Allen & Mitchell argue, for example, that the wide use of White middle-class students was not accompanied with further data making necessary distinctions in students explaining (explicating) research outcomes.

There are differences in students, culture and learning habits. Attribution theory, which refers to how students explain reasons for success or failure, has been used in a manner that ignores the differences in how Black and White children organize their casual world, especially in terms of success and failure. Sandra Graham, one of the leading scholars on African American motivation, argues that attribution theory is not un-useful, but the way it is used limits the inclusion of other significant factors in looking at school performance.

Most Black psychologists such as Jenkins, Parham and others argue that Black researchers have always emphasized the inclusion of context in motivational theory as essential. The African American experience has played a major role in adolescent worldview, norm development, values, and behavioral responses to social conditions. Blacks have had to deal with a caste system, cultural hegemony, and bad relationships in society. These factors have affected Black socialization, the adaptation process, and success in educational navigation.

Much of the past research on African American adolescents has approached the subject from the deficit model framework. This model tends to interpret test results from a negative in competent approach rather than from the adoptive process approach. The adolescent responds to a specific challenge context, in a particular way in a particular state.

Adelbert-Jenkins, a noted Black psychologist at New York University, reasons that in the past psychologists tended to view Blacks as social victims (in a negative light). Drive reduction theory, for example, viewed Blacks as being less motivated or passive in productive behavior. Self-esteem theory likewise showed that Black children felt ambivalent, at best, about themselves. But additional research showed that Black children of different social backgrounds had reported self-esteem levels at least as high as White children. Many motivation-related self-esteem studies have, in a sense, clashed in their findings. One part of the problem seems to be that Black children make use of multiple references and values when assessing their own psychological and motivational tendencies. This distinction cannot be made in many psychological tests. This means that utilizing qualitative methods would yield better information. Black adolescents also come to terms with their oppressive environment by imposing their own cultural forms. This is a motivational choice. It is a means to achieve a sense of competence in one's own domain.

There are other basic problems in comparing Black children and White children. Knight and Hill maintain that many research results should be called into question because the instruments themselves were developed in a majority culture. Many psychological constructs developed in and for the majority culture are not applicable across social and ethnic groups. Some theorists argue that the assessment of the validity of a test includes the consequences of use across groups. In other words, every test not developed in a specific context with group specificity should be reassessed for use in a different context.

This is true scientific research. Otherwise, unintended systematic variances can affect the results.

There has been needed criticism of motivational theory by Black scholars, but the theory-building (based on actual data) aspect of their work has been weak (Parham, White, & Ajamu). The question remains, should Black researchers pursue and correct White research weaknesses, or spend more time creating new paradigms and models for analysis? Graham has argued that many of the topics that have been researched regarding African Americans, such as conceptions of self and goal theories, have not been studied enough. Jenkins states that Black psychologists should avoid scrapping all the Western research on the psychology of Blacks and become more selective in their use of data. They should utilize data in a fairer assessment of African Americans.

In reviewing the literature, I felt certain key components were omitted, downplayed, overlooked, or underestimated in their importance to goal-setting theory in regards to African American urban males. These components can broadly be placed in the contextual category because they all involve interactions and responses to the social context. They are personal orientations that include the social dimension. All goals must be pursued in a given situation or social context. Goals will eventually confront and engage the relevant environment for realization and expression. Finally, there is the matter of how people really think. Do all adolescents or groups utilize the same patterns, learning styles and modes of apprehension of information in any given domain? Does the socialization process affect information processing? Do childhood developmental experiences form the basis for later academic performance?

Some researchers like Urdan now realize that the achievement context (including the classroom) plays a greater role in shaping motivation than was believed in the past. External goal structures that must be engaged by the individual will affect the goal process itself.

The components or constructs that have been selected for further study are relevant to the life, purpose, and motivational tendencies of urban, Black, male adolescents. They are social goals, personal values, well-being, and time orientation. All of these components also include a notion of the self and social as a part of motivational tendencies.

Gaps in the Literature: A Matter of Relevance

Social Goals

Social goals are defined as goals that have as a major component a need or desire to win approval, no matter what the other apparent goals may be. A student may strive for mastery, competence, or success in academic achievement, but he or she may also want to gain the approval of family, peers, teachers, or others in their social context. The student's cognitive process includes the appraisal of observing to relational others. Urdan and Maehr argue that the awareness of the social component of goal setting brings into motivational theory the influence of social relationships and social reality, which previously received scant attention.

I maintain that marginalized populations have had an ongoing need for social recognition as authentic persons. Society has a tendency to ignore the worth of the other as an integral, valued part of the social mainstream. This forces others into a position of having to reinforce, defend themselves in order to find acceptance by the larger society (LeCourt). There are persons who live in tension with mainstream society and with themselves. Part of the motivational life involves the redemption or reconstruction of the self. Some people had to rise above the label of "second-class citizen" or "invisible people" who were treated as nonbeings. The inclusion of social goals become a part of the goal complex. For example, the concept of the motivated self as the existential (coping) person has a strong social dimension. This person in the world must be considered holistically when evaluating his or her goal-setting orientation. MacDonald, Saltzman, and Leary argue that self-esteem itself is highly sensitive and responsive to social feedback and what is considered valuable to the self.

Inclusion of the social goal reinforces the notion of a multiple-goal theory. People can and do pursue more than one goal at a time.

One may have to achieve one goal to get to another. In fact, the concept of the motivated life includes a goal-lineage aspect. Often the need for social approval is a strong motivator no matter what other goals are present. Therefore, it takes the motivated life as a series of connected goals (goal hierarchy) to finally achieve wholeness as the truly actualized person in the world.

Student Persuasions (Values) and Goals

In the past, student-held values did not play a prominent role in goal setting in motivation theory. Yet values (personal persuasions) held by the self produce a sense of self. Selfhood, identity, confidence and goals are connected together. Steven Hitlin maintains that values have always been of interest to scholars but in relation to the self and society.

Values are really trans-situational goals that serve as guiding principles in the life process of the person. They contain elements of beliefs, end-states, and personal evaluations of behavior. Persons who have not yet developed their own value systems operate at a disadvantage. Values contain mental images and structures of the ideal. These principle ideas are more abstract than attitudes and operate across many situations. Values help authenticate the person. In fact, it is difficult to live with a diffused, unclear sense of values. These held ideas are central components of the person that link the person with his or herself inside of society. The linkage with others could be positive or negative, compatible or incompatible. Principle ideas help people to process information and play various roles. Values bring a sense of coherence, selfhood and motivated life. A sense of established selfhood can then add to one's sense of competence and outgoingness. The motivated, persuaded self then leads into the motivated confident life.

According to Graham and others, the belief system of African American adolescents does not always coincide with the values and normative beliefs of society. The unique values held by African American adolescents are important for evaluating their academic motivation. Values accommodate diversity of experience. They are a part of expectancy strivings, and cannot be separated from who the person is. Values affect relationships in society. In the past, minorities were studied with the intent of discovering how similar or how different their values were when compared with Euro-Americans. Even when Black adolescents fail in school, it does not necessarily mean they have lower values and lower expectations for success. Other factors often clash with their potential expectations. It is about how people see the world. Most people desire happiness, a role to play in life and a friendly responsive environment.

The periodically reviewed literature amply demonstrates the difficult relationship African Americans may have with mainstream society. The implications for Black adolescents are quite clear: Black adolescents need help in preparing to deal with wider society. People may exist on the same planet but live in different worlds. The motivated person is able to move beyond (not abandon) his or her culture into an interactive relationship with global society. The global society is here to stay. Developing personal values and striving for achievement is part of taking personal ownership for the future. The future involves successful encounters with many people.

Well-Being and Goals

One of the most important components of life for adolescents and adults is their sense of well-being. Vera Paster says that adolescents are into their culture, language, dress, taste, street activities, and, above all, the skill of coping. All of this contributes to their sense of survival and emotional well-being in the face of social challenges and hardships. The lifestyle of the urban adolescent is designed to avoid stressors. Create a personal enhanced appearance and gain public acceptance. Competence means a sense of personal security, confidence, and status in a given area or social role. It is to master a chosen role in the real world where the adolescent is respected.

Emmons and Kaiser report that emotional well-being involves thinking positively about the self and invoking social approval from others. This is a part of the coping style of striving individuals. It is a goal level that frames concrete and specific ways of living in a judgmental society. This goal relates to any other goal the individual may have, as goals interrelate as a system or network of goals involved in human striving. Or I would say, one moves into the motivated life and engages in the constant process of rebuilding, enhancing, growing the experiencing self with relational others. This also avoids the fragmentation of the self.

The role of meaning and existential coping is important in the concept of well-being as the individual is pulling his or her life together. Our lives are histories of episodic events and efforts to put ourselves together within a given time and context. Well-being is very important for goal setting and future status because it enables the person to function more fully and think more coherently. The person can have more social vitality if their psychosocial well-being is on a satisfying level.

How Far Can I See: The Future Time and Goals

Jennifer Husman and Willy Lens contend that students are chiefly motivated by the perceived utility of future goals. A student's sense of time and future perspectives develops over an extended period, as does the student's value system. Futuristic orientation is strongly related to a felt value system. As the student experiences life, existential meaning begins to emerge. In time, the student acquires a more abstract level of reasoning and the ability to process anticipated outcomes that are still in the future. Goals are located in the future as the student reflects in the present. The student is still living in the historic moment that informs his or her mood state. The student must begin to feel that he or she can handle goals and outcomes that are yet to be realized. The present moment can distort views of the future moment.

Without a positive view of the future there can be a greater tendency to eat, drink, and be merry now. Black, urban, male adolescents under oppressive conditions would rather engage in survival needs as a form immediate gratification. This way of life is often stigmatized in the literature. Some would argue that discrimination and poverty were so dehumanizing that some groups were overly preoccupied with the challenges of the present. Many individuals gave up or abandoned their claim on the future and even lost a sense of who they were. A positive future was distant, so subcultural life was developed in place of positive futuristic anticipation. A sense of well-being and "good times" was created through the emergence of rural and urban culture.

From Transformative Learning to Goal-Setting

Ryan maintains that motivation after learning stimulation is a phase of psychological development and transformation. The hierarchal pursuit of new interests results from the liberation of the bondage of survival concerns to ongoing human development. People begin to experience action flow and enjoy the seeking experience because they are in a sense renewed. Energy, direction and creativity are elements of motivation that moves beyond personal and social alienation. The informed person has an opportunity to direct his or her mind set or focus to more productive inquiries.

Transformative learning involves an affect (feelings or emotional) state of that brings energy and committed interest into the learners experience. Since all true learning is change in that something in the mind and understanding of the student is altered. In other words, learning affects the cognition organization of the mind and ways of thinking. This will be discussed later.

Graham argues that the process of setting and working towards goal fulfillment involves feelings. These feelings are in harmony with positive self-esteem. The person fulfills a sense of need in a given area. The person hopes for success. The person needs success. Low self-esteem brings with it feelings of depression. High self-esteem and a sense of accomplishment bring feelings of self-enhancement and approval from significant others.

The mood or state of the individual can change from depression, sadness, and rejection to feelings of adequacy and well-being. This is a transforming quality. The individual may have had positive feelings before a given accomplishment, but continued success leads the individual to internalize positive feelings as a more permanent reality. This again reflects the motivated life. The individual is less likely to need continual reinforcements to his or her self-esteem and can operate in a more independent way. This helps adolescents to learn how to cope better with life and reduce frequent mood changes.

Paul Tillich, the prominent scholar, says in his book *The Courage to Be* that people need courage in order to become. Becoming is a developmental quality. Tillich maintains that courage is the strength of social and psychological motivation, which is able to conquer whatever threatens the attainment of a desired goal. The individual engages in a goal-setting decision in order to seek for a significant level of existence as an act of faith. Positive feedback from related others is a type of motivating inspiration that support acts of *"courage to become"*. The individual is willing to make sacrifices and take risk because a supported state of readiness is experienced. The state of *"motivating courage"* creates movement towards self-development. The person moves beyond intimidating states of anxiety to a readiness to achieve.

Cranton says that transformation occurs during the process of critical self-reflection, not just personal reflection, which is limited. Deeper reflection involves a worldview or vision and a search for personal meaning in light of other mundane considerations. Deep self-inspection and reflection requires a broader spectrum and information repertoire. Meaning may come from the learner's perspective, which is often limited. Meaning may be imposed upon him or her by the dominant culture and may be negative. Usually public learning institutions are in synchronicity with the dominant culture. Transformational learning involves moving from the use of ideas from the dominant culture to use of ideas from the thoughtful visions of the learner. According to O'Sullivan the vision of the learner is not a reproduction of external ideas, it is a vision of the expanded new self. The expanded self integrates meaningful ideas from many sources, including the community, family, school, or spiritual. Adolescents need to experience liberating transformative ideas. Adolescents should draw upon an array of information that can contribute to their goal-knowledge and deeper perspectives. Personal goal-knowledge structure comprehends the dynamics of the motivated life.

Authentic learning experiences lead to new ideas. People learn something in the pursuit of chosen goals. Learning does not become transformative until the person engages in the process of coming to grips with what the new information means for them. After the learner engages in self-reflection, he or she is then able to explore future options and engage in action planning.

Marsick maintains that transformative learning is a significant process in preparing students for global higher-order thinking. First a student needs to think about his or her future in terms of locating or assessing the self. When a student reflects upon his or her future in the context of global society, he or she then creates a reflective opportunity to come to grips with the demands of the real world. When faced with reality, reflective students can develop various kinds of abilities and knowledge. The individual can make personal organizational changes that can lead to stability and positive future outcomes. The more the student learns and reflects, the more he or she can change. This implies operating in an environment that is conducive to reflection.

When a person faces an uncertain future, self-transformation is a necessity. The individual must gradually come to perceive the state of his or her self in relation to the world order. The individual arrives at a position that encourages the reshaping of his or her approach to future. The person is in a position to make the right choices because he or she is able to see the world as it is. The real world is larger than the self world of the individual. The person realizes that he or she cannot evaluate the world based upon narrow personal views and experiences. The transformation process begins when reflection begins. Marsick argues that the reflecting develops new action options, habits of mind, and new frames of reference. Transformative learning empowers the person to take self-corrective measures and responsibility for his or her own vision of life. The person is able to think through a comprehensive system of goal alternatives.

McClelland makes a major point that links collective motives and ideology. Whenever individuals engage in popular activities that involve a number of persons, the source of the motivation needs to be determined. People often do what "everybody else is doing." This is not personal motivation; this is ideology at work. Selling drugs, for example, can appear to be another form of motivation when it is, in fact, a socially driven act (with personal consequences). Street ideology has replaced personal, intrinsic, self-willed motives. The convenience of the marketplace engages a susceptible population. The origin of the motive is social and not personal. McClelland argues that prevailing ideology shapes the collective thinking of people. They then act upon a collective way of thinking. Sometimes people have collective needs, problems, and fantasies. In some cultures, even achievement "motivation" may be more social and cultural than individual. People can be ideologically driven. Those who are intimately (well-connected) and a part of that culture can manipulate its collective mind-set and views. This is one reason why we have politicians who feed distorted information and fear to the public about issues and positions. That which is presented in the environment becomes a part of the social matrix for individual responses to public discourse. The agenda for public focus and "significant" commentary on any subject is set by those whose interest lies within the social structure.

Autonomy, Freedom, and Goal Setting

Ekstrom points out that autonomy is more significant than freedom. Freedom during the civil rights movement in the 1960s essentially meant having greater access the social opportunity to participate in mainstream American life. This included fair housing, employment, political and educational opportunities. It also included the right to participate in all public institutional facilities. Franklin and Moss, prominent historians argued that freedom meant the opportunity to come out of the segregated, dehumanizing class to full first-class citizenship. Coloreds and Negroes soon became Blacks. Blacks became African Americans. These changes represented an intentional journey. I call it the collective motivated life towards self-acceptance, social recognition and full economic participation. The movement used the power of collective identity social-political cooperation and shared moral values to gain access to full participation in American life. Social access was seen as a major sign of equality and freedom. But there was more to life than having more of something. Freedom has come to mean that the person is "free" to select among the options made available to him or her without little personal input.

Ekstrom maintains that it is autonomy, not freedom that defines the person as a "free agent." A free agent always has alternatives and options to choose. The agent can take actions that emerge from the individual or the self; he or she can take actions that make a difference. Agency and autonomy is about sharing in meaning making and social innovation. It is not about reacting to options already crafted for public consideration. Agency is self-initiated action and decision making; it means to be self-governed.

Ekstrom argues that autonomy includes not only desire and want but the capacity to think and develop new perspectives and act upon them. Freedom then becomes an empowered position (state) intentional state that enables the person to act as a reflective agent in his or her best interest. In many ways, minorities now have freedom of participation in given areas. But many adolescents are living in a state of ambiguity and uncertainty. This study will show that some youth are living in a developmental slump. Adolescents in this state find it difficult to achieve well-being from the best sources. Having access to social facilities and still lacking the ability to access opportunities or make life-changing decisions is not freedom. Ekstrom has offered an important point about the ability to act as an intentional agent in your own affairs rather than reacting to another's agenda. Urban youth need to be counseled in the art of making the right choices and learning to access alternative views and careers that may not be apparent.

Goal-Setting Review Summary

This part of the literature review involved goal-setting theory. This review provided information on how the goal-setting process works. This process incorporates the needs and social situation of the individual who is in pursuit of some future state. The person reflects on his or her present and past experiences in the social environment. These experiences, needs, and social challenges are evaluated in terms of satisfying expectations for success and well-being. They are utility goals. Goal setting is choice behavior and the pursuit of expected rewards for personal effort. The review did indicate that African American student tendencies could not be reduced to broad constructs like the need for achievement, mastery goals, or intrinsic versus extrinsic motivation. These are categories and descriptions that don't always describe minority youth characteristics. Stipek, for example, states that goals are related to the thinking and personal value system of the person. If the person belongs to a non mainstream group, his or her goals and goal pathways might be quite different than the goal processing of most mainstream persons. The goal process, goal views, and goal knowledge structures are often subject to different influences. It is the context of adolescents in this study that help make relevant explanations of academic performance meaningful and better understood.

Goal-setting theory did not directly address the categories of personal values, social goals, future anticipation of success, and well-being in regards to some urban adolescent goal-setting tendencies. Goal-setting literature did help in the sorting out of the various ways of examining and applying goal-setting theory to urban adolescents. African American students tend to prefer task goals because they are not focused upon contrasting results seen in light of what other students may do. Mastery goals, for example, are less relevant to some students because mastery goals must serve an assigned utility purpose aligned to some meaningful purpose or task. Performance goals are usually designed to demonstrate ability and competence before others. Performance goals are not usually preferred by many students in many situations because they can be seen as too judgmental (Pintrich & Schenk). According to this study, select goals are often tied to the pursuit of well-being. The use of qualitative research helps to sort out what kind of goal-setting theory relates to the adolescents used in the study.

The question of why a goal should be set in the first place is important when interviewing urban adolescents. Information about performance feedback, the student's social position, and state of being is incorporated into the research. The availability of a support network, encouragement, and opportunity are considered with the thoughts and actions of some. Individuals may or may not change their way of thinking and acting if goal opportunities are present. The person must first integrate goal thinking into his or her self-system of daily life. In other words, McClelland argues that goals cannot be sustained if they exist outside of the person's normal thinking and behavioral patterns. Goals must a part of the defining self. There must be coordination and consistency of purpose and behavior.

Theories must be relevant to the life and cultural view of the student. The adolescent lives in and between two societal worlds (or more) which are reflected in the school system. The researcher must include the multifaceted reality in his or her testing procedures. This review was more involved that I wanted it to be; however, this information provided a wider window for a more complete examination of motivation in general and in groups in particular. A review of various approaches to motivation and goal-setting was helpful in pulling together and applying relevant information for this study.

CHAPTER 4
EARLY INDICATORS OF MOTIVATION TENDENCIES LESSONS FROM LIFE: SCHOOL AND SOCIAL SETTING

Going Where the Information Is

This study that we are about to discuss was important to my understanding more about the Motivated Life. It offered firsthand experience and information on the subject. There is no substitute for direct involvement in gathering real life data for further reflection and analysis. This research was vital in that it gave me a view of the early stages of adolescent motivational orientation. The presentation and analysis for the research data takes place in three parts. First there is a descriptive analysis of the school and neighborhood based upon county records. This will include information on the local urban community, the character of the school and student performance. This information is relevant to the goal-setting orientation of urban adolescents. The information on this social site will be contrasted with that on other high schools in the same city. Both the school and the neighborhood are major factors in how these adolescents respond to school educational programs and attitudes towards the future. The response to the research questions indicates what happens to the student when he faces school structures and social conditions.

The analysis then describes the researchers' school walk-through and on-site interactions during the school day. Conversations with school counselors and the school dean helped to present a more holistic account of the student-school academic relationship and support system.

The second part begins with a description of the pilot study. The pilot study was significant in that it indicated what the students thought about success. Student expressions and definitions about success helped the researcher to better understand the motivational tendencies of the adolescents.

The third part of the presentation in this chapter deals with the middle to high school transition. The data from the interviews demonstrated what educational difficulties there were in the transition process. Many students reported that their past and present school experiences affected their struggle to set goals. Their accounts will be presented and discussed in this chapter. The study showed that the first major theme concerning the students was about their state of readiness in entering high school. The next prominent theme in the research was that of getting out of high school. For many adolescents the challenge was not to do well but to survive the high school experience and get out.

The presentation and analysis in this chapter leads into a presentation in the next chapter about adolescent goal setting. This presentation provides data from high school adolescent student interviews. Interview responses show an emerging pattern of goal-setting tendencies in these adolescents.

The Social Context: The Neighborhood

The presentation of data for the study on urban Black male adolescent goal-setting begins with an overview of the local context, which includes demographics of the local community, information on the character of the school, and student performance. This section centers around the school, the student, and the student's academic participation in the school. Information about the nature of the school will also include interactions with school staff.

Kabara High School, the focus of the study, is situated in the northern part of the city and draws its student body from an area of about 9 square miles. It has on one side a modern track and field arena. Approximately 345,412 people live in the school's busy district. The total population of the city is 1.3 million people. In the study area 62 percent of the population is Hispanic, 29 percent is Black, 5 percent is Asian, and 4 percent is White. The unemployment rate in this area was 9.1 percent. Even before a major economic downfall occurred the unemployment rate for adjacent areas was 6.1 percent. The percent of the population receiving public assistance in this area was about 38 percent. The largest growing industry in this district is hospitals and nursing homes, which rose 2.4 percent during the year. Most other fields, except education, were stagnant or in decline. In the surrounding area there are 61 registered hospitals and nursing homes. Many of the parents of students involved in the study were employed in the health care field. Usually they were a part of the support staff, aids and helpers.

In regards to living conditions, most of the area consists of apartments and retail stores. Up to 35 percent of the land in this area contains multifamily units and 2.3 percent of the land is used for industrial manufacturing. Commercial and office use involves 7 percent of the land. Crime statistics, as officially reported by the county involved 7,396 rapes, robberies, assaults, burglaries, and auto thefts. There were also 44 murders in the local surrounding precincts. Quality-of-life complaints involved disorderly youths, excessive noise by residents, and rodent complaints in and around apartments. These precincts received many of the total quality-of-life complaints in the city. The precincts surrounding the school reported 265 persons were arrested for crimes involving guns and 5,341 persons were arrested for crimes involving drugs and narcotics during the study period. Constant arrests for drugs and narcotics were a part of the "normal" way of life in the area. During the same year, over 38,000 persons were arrested in the metropolitan area for drug-related offenses. The total represented 58.3 percent of those sentenced by the State for drug-related offenses during this period of time according to official records.

In the same community, however, there are also many life-supporting and cultural activities that help to increase the quality of life. The study high school had recently started a program using students to help tutor elementary school children at local community centers. A nearby college sponsors public performances in its arts center for the neighborhood. The district holds public forums on relevant issues like child abuse and domestic violence for members of the local community. There is a state program in the area that deals with juvenile delinquency.

There is a local midsize museum of the arts that sponsors public exhibits on such subjects like Brazilian history, the African American experience, Latino culture and other themes. There is a botanical garden for schools and the public. There are many senior citizen programs scattered throughout the area. There is a Jewish association of caregivers. The parks department offers free "senior fit" programs once a week. There are neighborhood enrollment sites for food stamps for anyone with demonstrated needs. The city provides limited youth employment services, HIV testing, Alzheimer's support, and antismoking programs. There are neighborhood community centers for both youth and adults. Child care programs of various types are a part of some of these centers. The local cemetery offers low-cost walking tours over the weekend for those who wish to examine significant memorials.

In total, there are 19 day care centers, four small libraries, four senior centers, and many youth development programs most of these programs must be sought by those who are interested.

Students and Their Environment

During the interviews the students expressed their feelings about actually living in the neighborhood in question. Neighborhood data indicated that the students lived in a high density-populated area with reported high rates of crime, drug arrest, and nuisances, including noise, rodent complaints, rowdy street behavior, and adolescent brawls in the streets. Interviewed students like Eston reported a sense of fear, frustration, and distraction while living in these neighborhoods.

Eston was age 17; his comments are fairly typical of the group's feelings. He reported:

> I grew up inside the house. There were too many gangs outside: the Crips, the Bloods, the Latin Kings. There were even Asian gangs. They attempted persuading me to join, but I resisted. I often heard gun shots at night. I have seen people get jumped and shot around my house. Eston stated during his interview: My cousin got raped and then shot 4-5 times when she tried to get away.

Community data also indicates the economic struggle and kinds of opportunities or lack of opportunities present in the geographical area. Eston lived with his mother and grandmother. His father left home. Eston reported that his mother was a nurses' aide working in a local hospital: "She is constantly working. She is not around too much." Eston, therefore, spoke more often of his grandmother who encouraged him. When asked about recent school progress, with particular reference to grades and attendance, Eston replied that he felt successful and his self-esteem was up: "I am serious about my work and I have been trying unsuccessfully to get a job, any kind of job. Right now, I am staying on track." Eston's grades fell from the 80s and 90s he was getting in a previous Catholic grammar school to 60 and below at Kabara High School. Eston said that no one in the high school seemed to care so he cut classes and wore do-rags to school even though it was against the rules. The teachers seemed aloof to him so he continued to slide until his grandmother's wisdom and counsel began to sink in. At the same time, Eston was observing the violence in the streets. Eston's average was still only 65 in the general program. Eston wanted to be successful and to be able to say, "I've done it despite obstacles."

William, who is in grade 12, also reported: "it is not the neighborhood it is the gangs…they shake others down, especially when they are bored." William, however, said he got himself together: "I have been able to concentrate on my studies". Most of the students in the study did not like conditions in their neighborhood.

The Study High School

This high school was chosen as the site of the study because it is a comprehensive public high school and contains the population, age group, and setting needed for the research. No entrance exam was needed for admission. The school has a diverse curriculum and various study programs. The school enrolled 4,350 students. At the time of the study, there were 1,499 in grade 9; 1,140 in grade 10; 762 in grade 11; and 613 in grade 12. The 613 12th grade students represented those who were left, out of approximately 1,200 students who entered as 9th and 10th graders (51 percent). There were 336 students who were not assigned to a grade because of incomplete work. This number of students could affect final graduation numbers. The student body was 44 percent male and 56 percent female. The school population was 60 percent Hispanic, 30 percent Black, 5.5 percent Asian, 4.2 percent White, and 0.3 percent Native American. The population of the school closely reflected the population of the surrounding neighborhoods. Approximately 240 (18.5 percent) of the Black students enrolled were in the college program, out of a Black population of 1,300 students. Some of these students were on probation in the program. There are three tiers to the college or honors program. Most of the Black students were enrolled in the bottom tier. There were about 1,200 students enrolled in the total college program. The highest tier was the advanced program for A students. Enrollment in honors programs is determined by grades and counselor recommendations.

In regards to state test scores, 64.3 percent of the students passed the English exam and 54.6 percent passed the math exam. In this city 57 percent passed the English and 51.4 percent passed the math for all the public high schools. In similar high schools, 65.8 percent and 57.2 percent passed the English and math exams respectively. The official graduation rate for the cohort class was 67.5 percent of the class. Citywide it was 53.4 percent. Students are given until August to be listed with their class after graduation. The school goal is to graduate students in or before five years. Those who received a Regents (state) diploma were 43.8 percent of the class. Citywide 27 percent received them, and in similar schools 34 percent received the state diploma. This seems to indicate that this high school is higher in academics than other comprehensive high schools. The graduation standard for the school is 55 percent of the cohort class. The dropout rate in the city was 14.1 percent for females and 18.6 percent for males. The Black students (male and female) dropout rate was 17.7 percent for all students in the city. The reported graduation rate for Black students in the study was 81 percent, or 275 students. These students received local diplomas by August 31. Depending on how the figures are accrued some information may be optimistic.

In addition to the general curriculum and the program for college-bound students, the school offers a health professions program, a public service program in law and government, and ROTC. There is also a business program for students interested in developing management or technological skills.

The economic background of the students consisted of the working poor, with 91 percent of all students eligible for free lunch. The public school average for similar schools was 48.7 percent. The suspension rate was 10 percent and 47.3 percent for similar public schools in the city. The average SAT score in this school was 888 and 864 for similar schools during this period. For selective public high schools where entrance exams are required, the average SAT score was 1,300. The average SAT score for area high schools was 915. This high school was an ideal site for the study in that it represented a balanced representation of students and programs in the urban setting. It was not an elite school, nor was it a lower tier school among the other high schools. When viewing neighborhood data, this school does fairly well in light of the contextual challenges students have to face and still make strides towards academic accomplishments.

School Administration

The school has a staff of one female principal, Ms. Gen Ammy, and three assistant principals. There is a dean of administration and seven department heads for foreign languages, mathematics, health careers, social studies, English, science, and special education. There are 21 counselors who work full-time or part-time, with some having teaching duties and substitution assignments. Students are randomly assigned to counselors except for those who may be in special programs. Some counselors work only in specific programs. Students are assigned to a program upon entry in the 9th grade. There is also a director of student affairs; this administrator oversees all clubs and sports activities. There are over 35 teams and more than 35 clubs in the school. There is one athletic director. About one-third of the students participate in clubs or sports. In addition to the administrative staff there are 217 teachers. The total school staff is made up of 305 persons, including office personnel, and security. The school was operating at 120 percent of its (space) capacity.

School Walk-Through

The school in this study is located on a plot of ground isolated from other buildings. It is housed in a large stately building and it has a campus-like appearance. There is no graffiti on the walls of the building. The grounds are well kept. The sidewalks surrounding the school are extremely clean and litter free. The adjacent community is, in contrast, an urban setting of heavy traffic, buses, trains, and crowded apartment buildings.

I made an appointment with the administrative dean for a walk-through of the school building in order to get a sense of the climate, dynamics, and organization that were present. The appointment was made for a Tuesday morning after the students had settled down. Most of the activity in the school is in the morning. School starts at 8:00 a.m. and ends at 4:15 p.m. There are ten periods in one day. All students do not start at the same time. The staff avoids appointments on Mondays because the beginning of the week usually brings too may problems for the staff to deal with. Students may have problems with other students, teachers, or with parents before leaving home, according to the dean.

There is a dress code which includes a ban on gang colors and head bands. No radios, Walkmans, cell phones, weapons, or drugs are allowed. No one is allowed in the school without identification and prior permission from an administrator. There is a peer mediation room in order to provide opportunities to resolve student conflicts nonviolently. A sign is posted on the wall as you walk in that states that a reward of $1,000 will be given for information leading to the arrest of gun-carrying students.

After school the students poured out onto the sidewalks and streets. They walked took buses or the train to a main avenue. I had a young photographer assigned to take pictures of the students walking down the streets into the nearby neighborhoods. But the photographer became afraid that the students might become offended at seeing him with a camera, so he would not take any pictures at all from any angle.

The building colors seem dark (grayish green) and the lights a bit dim. The building was large and old with four floors. I was able to view classrooms and speak to a few administrators and counselors on two walking tours. During the first tour I was escorted by the dean. The second tour I took while waiting for the dean, who had been called away because of a "crisis" that was happening in the building.

There were about 30 students in a class. The seating arrangements for each class were determined by each teacher in regards to self-seating by students. Most teachers allowed the students to choose their seating positions. During class changes the halls were filled with rushing, noisy students. But, in a few minutes, the halls were absolutely silent. The school was operating at 118.5 percent of its capacity. During the tour I was permitted to interact with some key staff members, including the director of student affairs and several counselors. I spent several hours in the counselors' main office. Part of the time was spent discussing student activities in the student affairs office. I visited the counselors' office on two occasions. I met with the dean on four occasions to talk about the school in general and to coordinate interviews with the students. The entire process took more than a year.

Student Interview Statements about Success

On recognizing that there appeared to be a pattern falling into place, the research analysis followed the trend that was present in the responses of the adolescents. The adolescents reported their own views on success and life. In dealing with goal setting in the data, the four elements found in the examination of the literature that appeared to be overlooked or undervalued were examined through goal-setting stages. These factors included: the role of well-being in motivation and goal setting, the role of the context of the urban student, personal values held by the student, and social goals and futuristic notions of success.

The steps or stages in the goal-setting process provided a natural means to examine elements of goal striving in the urban context. This included individual episodic life patterns related through the interviews. These are events that are meaningful to the adolescent. Responses to questions relating to success also provided the interviewer with a view of the social-educational orientation of the adolescent. After presenting the main theme, three in-depth examples from the interviews are first provided to add depth to the analysis. The examples will highlight the life experiences of the students, their sense of success or failure, school achievement, and personal values. The three students reflect different levels of academic and personal achievement.

Success as interpreted by the students in the interviews and pilot study was highly subjective and related to personal feelings about the students' social condition and well-being. This information is useful when school performance and goal setting is evaluated in light of the students in their social context. Gary reported during his interview: "Success to me is to be able to enjoy your future. Success is having good expectations and not having many problems or neighborhood problems. It is using your own imagination". In other words, Gary is idealizing and thinking beyond his context. Byzan is a student who was doing well, but he still defined success in general terms. Byzan stated: "I believe that success is to be yourself. I believe also that you get your mind on something and achieve, work hard, and do a good job in school." According to Byzan, success is also "getting out of high school," (but not with high grades or honors). Eston said, "To do what you want to do is success. It is not earning a million dollars; it is not being a computer person or a lawyer. It is feeling free." Eston wasn't doing that well, with a 65 average. Eston and Byzan saw success in terms of self-actualization and working hard; success is to do well to arrive at a state of felt freedom and autonomy. Neither of them viewed high academic achievement in school as a necessary guarantee for success. Tyson reported: "Success is to make a goal for yourself and work to the fullest extent to make it possible. You must work hard and study hard." Tyson realized that you cannot have success without hard work and study. Working hard seems to be a motif in the study. Most of the parents, especially the mothers, were reported as working long and hard.

Many students see success as an instrument to enhance their self-esteem. Oban said, "Success is to be all you can be. It is important to me to be something. I want to make an impact in society so people can see there is something to me." Oban's statement seems to reflect a need to be seen in a positive light. Success is seen as a way to affirm the self and offset stereotypic images of Black adolescents. William came from a background of near poverty. His mother was a store clerk, and his father was a cook in a small restaurant in another part of the city. He lived in a poor, violent neighborhood. William liked the messages in hip-hop songs about social struggle. William said:

> Success is prosperity. It is living a long life. Success is not letting anyone interfere with your goals. Right now, I am not successful. I don't have ten dollars in my pocket. I have to get money from my girlfriend. No one can look up to me. My self-esteem is low. It is a male thing. I can't even go to the movies.

Success to William involves financial stability, money as social capital, and self-respect.

Some students see academic success as playing a role in the need to strive for more important self-defining goals and to emerge from a degrading state of poverty or inadequacy. For example, Byzan said, "I believe in education for future success." Bordan said that he was concerned about his grades after "looking at life and hearing other people." These people spoke about their poor level of living. Bordan also said his own family was "in need for more respect from society." School achievement may be a tool for other expectations, like social acceptance and respect. The quality of schoolwork may suffer because the main interest and effort of the student is often applied to goals beyond the school. There must be a linkage between outside or personal interest and school performance.

The respondents did not speak in terms of outperforming others or striving for comparative superiority. The students were more reflective about their own social and economic status. For most of the adolescents interviewed, thinking about their conditions led them to think more about their future. The choice of engaging in learning and selecting goals involves deep-level information processing (Covington). Reflection often takes place about life before the student decides to undertake serious learning and goal setting. Eston had a 65 average and was content until he got tired of seeing street violence; that changed his attitude. In the interviews, he said, "my self-esteem is up. I am serious about my work." This type of thinking includes reflections on one's perceived social standing in the environment. During the adolescent pilot survey, one respondent spoke in terms of success despite problems, of "being yourself and being free." Another respondent said, "As you get older you see more of reality and you may decide not to strive for success." This is because it appears that society may be working against you.

Ogbu stated that parents communicate a glass ceiling in society which affects the children's school performance. Elliott and Thrash argue that real academic goals are centered around competence. But, in the case of the interviewed adolescents, goals are centered around life. Competence is developed in the pursuit of goals. Goal setting is the concrete means of making competence relevant. Before goals are set, the ideas of mastery, competence, and need for achievement are abstract.

Some researchers like McCaslin & DiMarino-Linnen argue that one reason why so much emphasis is placed upon competence in motivation literature and research is that Americans have been obsessed with power. Power orientation was more highly regarded than achievement itself. According to McCaslin the aim of power is to have an impact. The aim of achievement is to increase individual changes and change for success. When a person is seen as "competent" he or she can exercise the power of expertise and mastery over their less informed associates. One adolescent spoke about success as a tool for self-esteem and impacting society. Another respondent said that "success was getting out of the ghetto." He was speaking about the role of success in empowering social mobilization and ultimate respect. Some of the students continued to say that some of those who make it out of the ghetto and become rich and successful come back to the ghetto with status and respect. This kind of thinking is a reflection of social stigma and negative views about them that they must overcome. Some students felt they needed to overcome the stigma by being successful. Goal adoption is a means through which school achievement and motivation can build a sense of respect. School can help, for example, to facilitate competence, motivation, and goal achievement.

Middle School: Journey of Ambiguity

During the interviews with the students, some of the adolescents indicated that they did not accomplish much in middle school. The middle school experience was reported to be uneventful and unrewarding. This became a significant factor for most of these adolescents, who were placed in a general high school program. High school data showed that about 80 percent of incoming Black students were placed in low-tier educational tracks. Middle school preparation and academic performance determined how the student would be placed upon entry into high school. The students reported that during their middle school passage their grades and interest in school were mediocre in most cases. Few of these adolescents felt that they did well or learned very much. For the participants in the study, the passage through the middle school period almost was an invisible, non-stimulating gap in their lives. Few students could recall any role models, encouraging teachers, or major positive events. Few students felt a sense of achievement or success after the middle school period. There was little indication of serious goal formation during this period. The adolescents who were interviewed spoke about their school experiences just before they entered the high school.

Rhad, a senior in the general program who ranked in the 50th percentile, spoke about his experience in middle school as a playful period of unmotivated school performance:

I attended PS 68 Middle School. The school was OK. The teachers were OK. . . but they did not necessarily motivate you to achieve anything . . . I fooled around. I could play around without getting bad grades. Middle school didn't help me. My test taking skills are not that great.

Rhad admitted that he was partly responsible for his present plight because he played around and the school did not motivate him.

Swan, who was in the general program with a 77 average, said that he was still fighting laziness. He shared an overview of his middle school experience:

I have lived in the city all my life. I went to elementary school here. I attended middle school in the city. I live off 200th Street and Ham Road. I cannot think of anything interesting about the school I was in. I was an average student. I came to this school from my middle school and later became interested in computers.

Emil, who had two parents at home (both employed in a local hospital in low-paying positions), reported that his situation resulted from three factors: The middle school teachers were laid-back—non-motivating—his own laziness, and perhaps the turbulent environment. Emil admits that he was not challenged nor was he motivated enough to strive beyond mediocrity. Emil reported:

In elementary school my teachers encouraged me to do my schoolwork. In middle school it was different. My middle school teachers were laid-back, lazy. None of them inspired me. The last two years in high school (junior and sophomore years) were bad. I received bad grades. I was used to not doing anything in middle school which was easy for me. At the same time violence was going on in the school. A kid was stabbed, one was shot. There was a high police presence. The police were harsh on the Black boys but the White boys got way with more. The police really got upset about the way we wore baggy pants.

Middle School: Transition and Staff Perspective

When discussing the students' middle school experience, it is important to include the reported disadvantages of incoming students in regards to academic performance. The students would have to overcome this disadvantage during their high school career. This is doing double duty and carrying extra academic weight. The entry level of the students would affect the need for them to set early goals and increase both motivation and performance. The need for early goal-setting becomes even more urgent due to the fact that very often results show a greater testing gap between Blacks in high school and other students than occurred in the middle school (Nesbett). The catch up problem becomes worse under the exacerbated conditions. The future and well-being of the student is at stake. City test scores of 8th grade students entering the 9th grade were generally low. This presented a composite picture of many entering students. School counselors addressed the challenges of new students. This transition process is reflected in the chart on academic performance in the next chapter.

Counselor #1 spoke about how the students adjusted to the high school environment:

> Some students never adjust to high school. Freedom even with school rules is too much for them. This freedom goes to their heads. They can cut class if they want to. They can determine their own behavior. They can resist doing homework. They don't even have to talk if they don't want to.

It is possible that "freedom" is interpreted by the student as a lack of caring by the school. The school can take the position of "benign neglect" and ignore struggling students. Rhad (the student) mentioned, as already reported, that in high school: "They didn't care if you don't do your homework, they just fail you."

Counselor #2 spoke about the goals of the counselors. The main goal of the counselor is to see that students graduate in four years. The student is encouraged to attend classes, take the proper courses, get passing grades, and avoid behavioral issues. Students are encouraged to take responsibility for their own actions. Students are also advised that their perception of others and themselves and peer group issues in school affect how they act out their feelings and perceptions. The counselor argued that:

> One of the greatest sources of behavioral problems is the acting out of unexpressed feelings that are triggered by the least provocation. This leads to cutting classes, coming in late, or fighting. Many problems are carryover problems from middle school, where there has been a lack of help in social skills and handling conflicts. This is why there is such a high rate of 9th grade dropouts. The 9th grade reflects a continuation of many problems. Most of the problems are personal. The students are immature in terms of personal habits, scheduling, timeliness, social skills, peer problems, and conflict resolution. Once the student gets by the 9th grade he has a good chance of graduating.

In regards to dealing with entering students, the counselors reported that the main challenge the staff has in dealing with entering students is the students' inability to focus on external issues. The students are too involved with feelings and issues; they are distracted from the demands of the school. Counselor #2 said, "The achievement problem is not a school problem. It is a student problem. It is a problem of student focus. In addition, many did not do well in the past because of their heightened puberty. Their hormones were jumping."

Counselor #3 discussed the limited role of the school in assisting students: "Our job is to help the student when the student is ready to be helped."

School counselors have made it clear that "it is not the school's responsibility to provoke goal-setting, motivation, futuristic concerns, academic ambition, or serious attitudes among students. If this happens it is incidental to the purpose of the staff, which is to help students finish school according to the desires the student already has. The staff is not the "cheerleaders section" of school life. Maintaining good high school performance is the responsibility of the student. The counselors and staff are present to assist, guide, inform, and help schedule the student with appropriate courses according to his or her tested abilities and desire. The individual student "is not the personal responsibility of the counselor."

Counselor #3 said that the counselor's job:

> is to help the student find his or her way through the school system. It is to help the student to have a sense of direction in regards to school life. The more aggressive the student is the more likely the student is to get a response from any staff person. Of course, many students are very fragile in that they give up easily. They are easily discouraged.

Counselors see themselves playing an official role of guiding and enabling. In addition, students who are labeled as drifters, uninterested, lazy, or underperforming are less likely to get serious attention from counselors who are overloaded with 250 to 300 cases per year. In a large sense, the student is responsible to show professional others that he or she is serious enough to merit a serious response from staff. There is occupational and college counseling for those who have already decided where they want to go or are on a particular course of pursuit. William reported that "counselors give you good advice when they have time. They don't insist on seeing you. If you are doing bad, you have to insist on seeing them weekly." William said that "counseling is a relationship". Eston said, "The counselors were helpful but talked mostly about scheduling classes". Peterson commented that "counselors will not get into your personal goals but will talk to you about college only if you are in a certain program, like the College Program". Students are not always aware of the importance of future preparation. Most of them are involved in personal, family, and economic difficulties. Neighborhood data shows that a large percentage of the population is on the borderline of poverty. At least one-third of the population receives some kind of public assistance.

Most of the students in the interview had similar contextual experiences. Urban life is challenging, and often violent and confrontational. Only a few students were able to translate challenge into performance for a better future. The adolescents generally needed strong prompting to get serious with their studies. Help is needed for the student to see school as an aid and instrument to success. The school position is that help is available to those who have become interested in the school itself as an educational resource.

The middle school is important because it helps prepare the student for his or her high school experience. The success of the student in high school is threatened if the students do not have a strong academic and social base of departure (San Antonio). Rhad said, "middle school didn't help me and my test taking skills are not that great." Successful transition from one environment to another requires social, psychological, and emotional readiness. Rhad also reported, "my self-esteem is mediocre and when I do something stupid like failing something it goes down further". The added burden of having a weak economic and social background adds to the difficulty of having a strong starting basis for the possibilities of a successful high school career. Energy is then invested in merely adjusting and surviving rather than achieving. The chance of starting high school in honors classes is less likely and the chance of being enrolled in a more general course track is more likely. The student is also likely to end up in a lesser cohort of entering students and peers. Therefore, the student begins his or her high school career reinforcing educational inequalities with a valuable loss of time and motivation. The student is almost structured into a particular trajectory. The student now must come from behind in order to have an acceptable academic finish in four years, or usually five. Greater effort is needed to catch up and perform well. Becoming a student, in reality, is a goal in itself. This is why Respondent #4 said that: "going to school was success in itself."

Getting Out of High School: Lowered Expectations

During the interviews there were several interviewees whose emphasis or stated goal was to finish high school. Getting out of high school almost became a preoccupation. A great sense of urgency emerged as the students struggled with poor or average academic performance. Even with a few good students the emphasis was still to get out of high school. During conversations with school counselors, this theme again sounded. The counselors stated that it was their duty to help the student get out of high school. They reported that this message was an important part of the counselor's advice to students. The message sounded very positive. Tyson talked about getting out of high school. He said: "They (my family) remind me of how hard it is in the world. I am trying to get out of high school. I have no particular goal besides getting out of high school". Themos said: "I want to finish high school at least. I don't like school." Peterson reported, "I have had a lot of good teachers and counselors in the past. They encouraged me to focus on getting out of high school".

Several counselors reported their official and personal feelings about the role of the school and the counselor. Counselor #5 spoke in general terms. He said that "the task of the counselors is to facilitate the social and academic development of the students. . .It is our goal to connect them to resources that will provide aid via counseling". Counselor #2 reported that: "the main goal of the counselor is to see that students graduate in four years, attend classes, take the proper courses and get passing grades".

On the surface it would seem noble to encourage good and struggling students to finish high school: it is something they have to do. However, this perspective seemed a bit parochial or narrow if the student has the ability to do better, whatever his average. Very few students reported that they were encouraged to excel or graduate on a higher academic level. The advice to get out seemed to be a convenient exit strategy. This theme of getting out of high school appears to reinforce a survival mind-set. It seems to cater to the weakness or lowered expectation of the student. There are risks involved with just graduating with little or less regard for academics, class rank, or future preparedness.

In the study, 80 percent of the adolescents were enrolled in the general program. The majority of the Black students enrolled in the college program were assigned to the lower third of the program. Kerckhoff argues that in today's world just having a high school diploma actually depresses the attainment of young high school students. Since high school diplomas tend to be generalized and unspecific, they have little value. They are not usually occupationally relevant. If the student, especially the Black student, does not have technical preparation or vocational training, finding work will prove to be difficult. Kerckhoff says that without institutional guidance or support there will not be a linkage between a high school diploma and employment in the local labor market. This throws the rationale of "just graduating" into a whole new light.

This raises the question again of what the purpose of high school is in the first place. I argue that high school, like adolescence, serves the function of preparing the individual for adulthood and life in the real world.

Carter reports that it is the purpose of high school to catapult the student into a new world both academically and socially. High school must be completed. However, the bigger picture must not be obscured. Most of those interviewed who spoke about college were not in the school's college program. There are risks in operating in a solely survival mode without a sense of participation in a structured purposive program. Specific readiness is needed to address the personal future of the student. If the student has not envisioned possible goals or aspirations beyond high school, how much meaning can high school have? If there is no sense of student purpose or direction, what will drive his personal motivation?

Themos, whose mother died when he was young, lived with his father. He said that "he is not really moving towards anything. . . my father just went back to work at Verizon after six months of being unemployed."

High school should have utility value since the presence of goals informs student behavior. Setting goals in high school does, in fact, influence school achievement, depending upon individual subjective purpose (Covington). Having goals while in high school helps the student to engage in self-regulation and to participate to a greater extent in his or her learning process. Students with goals tend to focus more on school demands, assignments, and needed personal resources for high school achievement. The quality and level of commitment and performance rises in areas where goals have been set. Even the student's sense of well-being is affected, because a revised self-evaluation includes higher performance and rewarding strategies that are starting to pay off (Kaplan & Maehr).

A Journey of Personal Responsibility

During the study students spoke about the freedom they experienced in high school. Byzan said: "I like my school because it is a good school with lots of freedom." The students generally could go out to lunch, attend class, cut class, take homework lightly, and choose to see their counselors if they wanted to. If the student was not motivated and keenly aware of the social perils of under-preparation, they could set themselves up for failure in life. Counselors expressed their opinions as was reported. They said in short the student is responsible for his- or herself. At some point, there needs to be a point of activation and stimulated interest in the future. The adolescent begins to take steps in order to advance towards a sense of real progress in goal setting. Some adolescents realized that sensing personal freedom in school was not the same as feeling free to move on, or being enabled to perform on a higher academic level.

Bordan reported:

> Up until high school there was little to motivate me to do any thing but to attend. I did not really put any attention to getting good grades until last year or my second year in high school. I did just enough to get by. My average was Cs and Ds.

Themos stated: "Success is doing something you want to do. It is not being forced to do what others want you to do. My parents got upset when I cut classes but they had no control over me." Themos began to realize what he needed to do: "You must go to school. While you are in school you need to find out what it is you really want to do. Then you need to map it out".

Oban related his past indifference:

> The next day if I don't have the homework to turn in the teacher just looks at you and says nothing. They mark it in a book. I would rather that they say something. When the teacher says nothing it makes you more lax.

Oban was looking for provocative encouragement. School counselors made pointed statements about student responsibilities. Counselor #3 said:

I don't think that it is the counselor's job or teacher's job to provoke the student to wake up about life and get serious about goal setting and education. This they have to do on their own. It is their responsibility. When it happens it happens. Our case load is heavy. It is between 250 to 300 students per counselor. Some students don't get here at all and others I only get to see sporadically. Our job is to help the student when the student is ready to be helped. Some students opt to join the military. I have personal negative feelings about the military but I would not try to talk students out of joining if they want to. I don't think it is the best decision to make. Students sometimes join when they have nothing else to pursue. They don't have anything else in mind. So with a little encouragement they join. There is a lot of push from recruiters.

"Whenever they get to the stage they want help they take advice more seriously. When the student starts thinking about graduation they become receptive to information about school requirements and they start to take testing and passing seriously." Counselor #2 said:

Students are to take responsibility for their own actions. Some students are too involved with feelings and issues that they are distracted from the demands of the school. The achievement problem is not a school problem. It is a student problem.

Students and Staff in Contrast: Summary

Interactions and on-the-spot interviews were conducted with three counselors, the academic dean of students, and the director of all student activities, which included 70 teams and clubs and many special activities. Much information was gained about the school, its policies, and expected student roles. About seven formal and informal visits were made to the school through the academic dean, who had also been a counselor himself. This does not include drive-by observations undertaken to view students entering and exiting the building.

The data from the interviews with both staff and students shows a remarkable contrast in views about the role of the school for struggling students. As the data has shown, many Black male students were struggling with mediocre grades, maintaining an interest in school, and any possible futuristic expectations. Many of them arrived from middle school with disadvantages, such as poor preparation and uncertain feelings about completing their high school career, without any special interest or purpose in mind. More information on this uncertainty is demonstrated in the data on goal-setting tendencies to follow.

Many students who were experiencing achievement (grade) problems reported in the study that counselors tended to concentrate on scheduling classes and dealing with course conflicts. They also tended not to want to get involved with personal goals or future plans unless the student was already enrolled in the honors program. The main emphasis was to encourage the student to do well enough to get out of high school. There was little challenge or push by most teachers if the student lacked in his class performance, according to student reports.

The counselors and the dean of students who were interviewed in-depth about school policy in helping struggling students general replied by placing responsibility for achievement performance on the student. Several counselors generally felt that:

> Students have many personal and social problems when they arrive. Some students never adjust to high school. They can't handle freedom. Students are too immature in their habits, scheduling, and time sensitivity. Our job is to help those students who are ready and to get them through the system. The students need perseverance. They need to read the school's rule and policy manual. We try to connect them to resources.

The director of clubs, sports, and events said: "More students need to join some kind of activity. This gets them more involved with the school itself." In short, the staff said that it was the student's responsibility to get disciplined, learn the rules, and concentrate on their schoolwork. The school staff felt it had a clear understanding and approach to students who did not have a strong sense of direction, commitment, and achievement.

Some students in the study expressed a need for personal help or encouragement to perform better and move towards success. The staff that was interviewed said it was not the school's responsibility to engage in motivational activities or personal guidance beyond facilitating school completion, career instruction, proper programming, and college information for college-bound students. The dean, counselors, and special activities director all stated that they were glad to assist students who were open and ready to take schooling seriously. However, the counselors also said that "They were not there for personal intervention." Any nonacademic concerns were referred to the social workers (service) department by the counseling staff.

Summary Charts:
The Journey

Middle School – High School rites of Passage

Getting out of High School:
Dynamics of the Study

- Avoid total failure: Get in, Get through, Get out
- Find your own self: Past State, Present State, Future Goals
- Find good advice: Informed informers, Advocates
- Middle School Performance: Set the Placement Stage
- High School Track: Deterministic Rules Already Set?
- Continuing education: un-educated or New Mindset
- Get a life: get a job, stay out of trouble, get serious, set goals
- Success: Not the path of least resistance, get a new time orientation: Achieve!
- "Connect the dots": learning paths, choice-making, self-regulation

---

Existential Reality

Some Urban Male Students Tendencies

Academic Dormancy – Laxity – Inertia – Paradoxes

Contextual – Cultural Absorbtion

Self-History – School History

Diffused Focus – Motivational Ambiguity

The Journey

CHAPTER 5
PUTTING THE PIECES TOGETHER:
EMERGING PATTERNS
STRUGGLING TOWARDS
THE MOTIVATED LIFE

Discovering Goal-Setting Tendencies

In the previous chapter, a description on how the study began started with an overview of the neighborhood and high school that the students in the study attended. The investigation included contextual information about the urban setting where the students lived. Information on student performance, school structure, and community characteristics were reported. This data was important because it provided information about the conditions under which students had to being their motivated lives. Educational institutions, neighborhood conditions and stressors can impact upon how people struggle to enact a motivated life. School-community data helps provide better understanding about factors that lead to deeper adolescent participation or withdrawal from academic and social life. Adolescent and young adult orientation can be described in terms of everyday environmental experiences.

After viewing the contextual data of adolescents in the study and the conditions under which they live, this chapter emphasizes the details of the adolescent's response to his urban experiences. This chapter addresses the personal orientation of the students and how they intended to deal with the future. The interview responses in this chapter all center around goal-setting tendencies and strategies of success. Thus, we move from context to goal setting. Goal-setting theory has broadened to include both context and personal tendencies.

Related to the study on goal setting is information on factors such as success hindrances, social goals, family participation, future orientation, and hip-hop music. These factors will be analyzed and discussed. This information helps to provide a more complete understanding about goal-setting orientation in Black urban male adolescents.

Educational Narratives: Coming to Grips with Setting Goals

The purpose of the interviews was to provide information that would show any themes that might be present in the responses of the students in regards to goal setting. This part of the study begins with three interviews of students who differ in academic achievement and goal-setting orientation. One is an average student in school. Another student is doing fairly well. The third student is a high achiever. The interviews indicate some of the factors that affect goal setting and performance.

The first student is Swan. Swan was in the general program. He had a 77 average. Swan was just an average, laid-back student in middle school. Swan gradually became interested in computers. His mother gave him one at the age of 10 or 11. Swan wanted to enter the computer field or even become an engineer or maybe a businessman, but his grades were not consistent. Swan went through periods of laziness. His father was helpful but he lived in Florida. Swan struggled with getting into a consistent flow of study.

Swan did have an 85–90 average in his computer courses, but his other course averages were low. Swan had taken computers for three years in high school. Although Swan had not applied to any college (and he was in the 12th grade) his attitude was good despite his home life. Swan did not see his mother as often as he would have liked.

She worked in a nursing home. But his mother and grandmother encouraged him nevertheless. He had a younger brother and sister. His mother talked to him about cutting classes and passing subjects other than computers. These talks were encouraging but not too effective because his mother worked so much she could not follow up on his school performance. Swan said that his self-esteem was high. He had high confidence in his skills. But high self-esteem and inconsistent performance work against each other. This hindered the progress Swan could be making.

Swan had a lot to overcome with his general high school record. Even if he did better in his senior year, it would not raise his GPA very much. His family income was limited because his one parent who lived at home was employed in a low-wage occupation. But, in regards to personal goals, he could succeed in the computer field. He could either go to a community college eventually or get a job and look forward to college later. Swan said the school had encouraged him to graduate and get a diploma, but not to excel. Swan had an obvious track record of studying and achieving in the computer field. He did have initiative. But he did not possess good self-management skills. His regulatory behavior (discipline) was poor. At the time of the study, he was looking for a job. Swan may have been afraid of the academic challenge of more schooling. He had moved beyond pinpointing his interest in computers to slowly putting together a self-assigned task of working any place he could. Swan said, if he could, his "second choice is to go into business or into marketing." With a little help and encouragement he will move beyond his weaknesses in high school. He was struggling with having a strong, specific goal. He can be successful if he is willing to follow through with one single goal.

The second student, Byzan, is struggling to get ahead. Byzan spoke about his personal history. Byzan had an 87 average in the general program. He was 16 years of age and in the 11th grade. Byzan attended elementary and middle school in the city. Byzan said that middle school was dull and boring. He could not remember any interesting events in his middle school history. The teachers he reported were nice, but they did not encourage him. They did not ask him any questions about his goals or aspirations. When Byzan visited his counselor on a weekly basis, it was mostly: "hi and bye." The visits consisted mostly of scheduling comments and nothing about his future aspirations. The visits lasted about seven minutes. There was no push, challenge, or incentives coming from the school staff. Byzan said he spent 45 minutes a day on homework and 28 hours a week watching TV. He was on the track team and lived with his father because his father could support him better than his mother could. His mother worked in a hospital and had experienced a great economic struggle. His father lived in the city and worked for the city. At the time of the study, his mother lived in a near-by suburb. Byzan said that his father told him education was important. Byzan also said that it took a while before that meant something to him. He began to realize something was missing in his school performance.

For a while Byzan thought about becoming an MD. He said, "I couldn't handle all that goes into becoming an MD," so he dropped the idea. "It seemed like it was too heavy of a goal." Byzan said,

> There were so many things that I thought about to myself. When I got to high school I realized how much I did not know. I had very little confidence in myself. I have no goal in mind right now except to go to college. I thought about a business career in medicine, like selling medical supplies and running the shop. I thought about being a sports manager. I believe in education for future success. I have an 87 average in the general program. I am behind in English. I am doing well in chemistry and math…

> The biggest disappointment for me was the separation of my mother and father. It was a difficult time for me. I don't like school violence (mostly from immature and touchy freshmen). I have no complaints about my neighborhood but there are a lot of cops around on every block because there is much violence and drugs. But I don't hang out. I listen to rap artists such as Jay-Z, R Kelly, 50 cents and NAZ.

Byzan had to deal with many personal and social factors that bothered him. These factors obviously interfered with his ability to concentrate on his future and excel in school. He repeated the same "getting out of high school" theme. That was probably one reason Byzan defines success as: "Setting your mind on something, working hard, and achieving. It is doing a good job in school. It is getting out of high school."

Byzan seemed to have good qualities. He was interested in education. He had a good average, but he was still assigned to a general program. Byzan said his homework was easy yet he was concerned about getting out of high school and having a lack of confidence in himself. Byzan and others helped to reinforce the emphasis of external motivational incentives for Black adolescents who need external encouragement or rewards. Somehow Byzan did not communicate his thoughts to anyone about becoming an MD; perhaps it was because of his past mediocre record. Maybe this was why he couldn't get beyond earlier failures. Byzan needed others to give him a push and personal encouragement to cheer him on, so to speak: "No one except one teacher seemed to have had any interest in me or pushed me to do anything."

The third student is called Pinnock. The Pinnock family presents a different perspective on a Black family. Pinnock was 14 years of age and a freshman at Karbara. He had attended middle school not far from Kabara High School (about two miles or less). Pinnock reported that his middle school experience was good. He said:

> I liked my middle school experience a lot. It was pleasant. My teachers were very helpful. They gave me personal attention. Whenever I acted out in class or had a problem the teacher came and spoke to me. We had a good relationship.

Pinnock had an 89 average in middle school and a 95 average in Kabara at the time of the study. He was admitted into the college program from his middle school. Ninety students from his school were admitted into the college program out of more than 1,000 who applied. Pinnock was still rejected from a city honors school because his scores were not high enough. There was too much competition.

Pinnock said he had a successful transition into the high school because: "My parents were talking to me all the time so it didn't hit me as hard as it did others. I was born in the city but my parents were born in Nigeria. So they were always cautioning me." Pinnock had middle-class parents. His father was a probation officer and his mother was a social worker. Pinnock said, "I would like to attend Vassar College, but I also like NYU and Columbia in New York."

Pinnock was not only in the college program, but he was in the top tier (the third advanced tier). This was rare for a Black male adolescent. Pinnock has the social skills and the mental attitude to attain his goals. He already was talking about significant colleges at age 14. He wanted to be an actor (of all things). Pinnock said: "I want to be an actor. I joined the drama club in middle school. I continue to attend a neighborhood drama club while I am in high school. They meet at a nearby charter school after school". We shall not know if he changes his goals later.

The professional background of his parents and their instructions to him over a period of time has made a difference in his setting "firm" goals by the 9th grade.

Pinnock exhibited several steps in the goal-setting process. He had a high awareness level of the need to set goals, and he was very thoughtful and informed about goal-related opportunities and the need to follow up. He made the effort to join a drama club. He knows about the better schools. He knows about society but says, "Success is achieving long-term goals. Success is learning from your family."

Obviously Pinnock had the advantage of having educated parents, economic stability, and more detailed instructions and guidance in his home. Success was modeled right in his house. Pinnock did not need to react to episodic events to remind him to take life seriously. This example seems to fit the model Ogbu, the educational anthropologist, sets forth in emphasizing that negative parental communications hinders the thinking and motivation of a child. The right information coming from parents can encourage the child who especially has social and economic advantages. Pinnock avoided peer pressure by staying in an upper-track program in school and by involving himself in more middle-class activities. His peer group in the advanced program was much different than those in other programs. He didn't participate in any sports or clubs in the high school. Pinnock said, "You have to create your own support group."

Student Interviews: Emerging Goal-Setting Patterns

Analysis of these interviews shows a pattern of phases in the goal-setting process. The three students were at different phases in their future planning. Only one student was sure of himself. Two of the students were trying to "get out of high school." These adolescents generally became serious about their studies and goal setting after they had gone through a period of lethargic indifference and apathy. The adolescents reported that they gradually began to realize what state they were in and thought about the future. The third student came into the high school 9th grade with a goal in mind. His middle school teachers had encouraged him. This was a type of push. These student reports ranged from apathy to serious planning.

Other students reported similar trends. Themos reported that prior to entering high school, "I became lazy. I cut my classes. I did not do well...I'm trying to find out what I want to do. I want to finish high school at least". Themos seemed a bit melancholy as he reflected on his past.

The students moved towards making a decision after it became apparent to them that they were not going anywhere. Tyson said, "I have recently gotten serious about education. I was just getting by...I wasn't making any effort before to do better...I go in (to my counselor) check grades and things like that...my family made me interested in my future". Tyson sat slumped down in the chair. He didn't seem to have a lot of self-confidence. He seemed to be sad and frustrated.

The students began to name possible goals or aspirations that could become goals. At this stage of reflection, the adolescents not only named a goal but some of them followed up by making some effort to get more information, improve grades, study more, and invoke the counsel of others in the process. Some students went beyond seeing the counselor for grade or schedule checks. Carlin, for example, was in the pilot study but he was also among some students like Tyson who decided to move beyond complacency to a more serious pursuit of education and goal setting.

Carlin stated that:

> Now I go to see my tutor. I do at least 30–45 minutes of homework each night …my goal is to be a judge… I am striving to pull up (my grades), that is why I am now going to see a tutor regularly.

(I later wondered if the prominence of going to court in the neighborhood influenced Carlin's desire to be a judge.)

Some students continued the process by adjusting their lifestyles, scheduling classes relevant to their goals. They began to act out on a continuing, persistent basis the desire to change their failing or mediocre academic performance and implement an action goal-sequence made up of definitive steps.

Bordan, who was in the 10th grade, said:

> My average was Cs and Ds, but looking at life and hearing other people caused me to get serious…last year I began to ask my cousin who was going to college for help. I thought about going into business for myself…I have also thought about going to George Washington University in D.C…Yes, I am willing to make the adjustments to go to college. I expect to be in college in about five years from now.

Bordan is beginning to have a sense of urgency about his future.

One student in the study had actually been admitted into a college; others accomplished some necessary prerequisites that would most likely lead to goal fulfillment. In other words, making significant progress in pulling together some sub-goals first put the student in a much better position for his future well-being and success. Peterson, for example, was a senior in the college program. He was 17 years old. He lived in a neighborhood of gangs and violence. He lived in a crowded 300-unit apartment building. His parents were divorced. His mother worked two jobs in nursing at a local hospital. She said to Peterson, "You have to do better than me." Success to him was about well-being or being satisfied with himself. Peterson loved computers and translated that love into pursuing a technical career. He is an example of having a goal and achieving it. He had been accepted to City Technological College. Peterson's love of computers motivated him to take computer-related courses and do well. His GPA was 80.

Peterson is a good example of how select factors in the study emerged during the research. The role of well-being, personal values, social values, and the student's view of his future worked to motivate him to move beyond his turbulent environment. Peterson valued learning and planning for the future. Peterson was determined to make it. His neighborhood conditions, his mother's struggles, and his personal views motivated him. His future perspective of success led him to select classes in line with his goals for college and computers. His friends had already started calling him "college boy." Peterson stated, however, that his school counselors only encouraged him to "focus on getting out of high school".

Peterson went through several stages. The first stage was the existential or reflective state. This state defined where he was located in terms of time and accomplishment. After he realized his plight, he moved on to work out his goals.

Eston, for example, reported that he was trying to come out of a bad state of laxity. His neighborhood was violent and full of gangs. His mother, a nurse's aide, was struggling to survive. She worked all the time. He rarely saw her. His father had left home. He was an unemployed construction worker. Eston's grades fell from the 80s and 90s in a previous catholic school to 65 in high school. He felt that his teachers were aloof and his counselors were only concerned about scheduling classes. Eston also felt that society was indifferent or neutral in regards to helping people. Eston said that success was: "being able to say that you have accomplished something despite the obstacles." This is how he saw life—full of obstacles, full of violence and trouble. Most of his friends were in gangs. Eston was in the 11th grade with a poor average in the general program. At the time of the study, he said that he had begun thinking about his future. At the same time, he was in a general, non-specialized program late in his high school career. This, in itself, didn't really prepare Eston for anything in particular. At the time of the study, Eston said that he was staying on the right track with grades and his school attendance.

Eston did not want to let his father down. He said: "I am serious about my work. My self-esteem is up".

After the students are perceived as being indifferent or lazy, they begin to reflect this. This stage is the thinking stage. Thinking is the first step in setting any goal (Carver & Scheier). The adolescent must engage in a mental activity of scanning, selecting, and imagining a desired state of well-being. This is exactly what these students did. The student assessed himself and his immediate world. The adolescent makes use of what is known (Kruglanzki). Goals have a beginning, a life, and an end (realization). Thinking involves reflecting on ideas about self, the environment, the economic state of parents, and the possibility of a failed dead-end life. Peterson, Bordan, and Eston thought about their environment, family conditions, and what the future could look like.

The thinking process involves the thought out need to make a decision about something. Eston said that he decided he wanted to be something after reflecting on a turbulent, nonproductive life. The second step occurs when the adolescent decides to do something about his future. Carlin said that he had to "avoid pressure from others so you can be yourself." His aunt encouraged him to reflect on how well he was doing. He only had a C–D average that had become about 70.

To name a goal or desired future state involves the process of choosing; this is the naming stage. This is a decisive step. Naming needs to be concretized. Naming ought to involve anticipation and expectation. Carlin said he wanted to be a judge and went to see his counselor—"but she didn't take me seriously. She did encourage me to bring my grades up. She didn't talk to me about anything beyond high school." Carlin did take this advice and he is doing better. The adolescent began to sense the need to declare some kind of goal. Naming ought to give direction to doing. Naming can be a therapeutic or redemptive act. It can be an act of self-encouragement to avoid a sense of non-worth or failure. Naming a goal helps to create personal meaning. Naming could be an aspiration, a desire without effort or commitment. Under the right conditions or push, the student can move beyond naming to pursuing.

Project assignment is the self-appointment of a goal as a task to be pursued as confirmed by goal effort. The adolescent determines that his choice becomes a must do activity. Rhad said, "I hope to get a degree at some point after high school. I hope to become an actor on TV".

The expressed goal became a part of the ongoing thinking of the adolescent. Rhad belonged to several drama clubs. He had already started on his future role by getting involved with programs in the school that helped to reinforce his stated goal. He made a project out of his goal choice. He was engaged in school-sponsored plays in the neighborhood.

There must be effort and action that is incorporated into the life pattern of the person. Goal effort could include consulting with others, doing personal research, or creating a goal strategy or a plan of action. All of these acts and more constitute goal development. Goal effort means that sub-goal initiatives have begun in the goal hierarchy. Rhad went to see his counselors. They gave him a plan. His counselor said: "You must pass all of your courses or you will only be allowed to take basic stuff."

Goal persistence involves lifestyle changes and the adoption of a means to carry out the project. This action shows that the goal-setting process is continuing and the student is deeply involved in getting control of his future. Rhad began to distance himself from his friends who wanted to influence him. He said to them, "You live your life and I will live mine." This is a part of goal commitment and continuance. Rhad's grade average was now B to a B+. He was working to rise in his class percentile. Rhad realized that he needed a better academic record to achieve his goal and further training.

There were students in the study who saw the importance of effort. Some of them, like Monk, Byzan and Tyson, said that: "success was getting your mind on something and working hard to achieve your goals." Students can be very realistic in attributing success, good grades, and academic progress to personal effort. They did not blame others for a poor performance. The literature sometimes indicates that Black students do not assume responsibility for their poor school performance (Cokley). The students felt they could experience academic success, but in this study most of them usually attributed their failures or poor performance to personal laxity. Even if the student received little or no help from the school they recognized their own failures. This was an indication that the student was taking personal responsibility for his life. Monk said that: "Success is not being hard headed and listening to negative people ... success is hard work ... don't wait on others to help you."

Byzan said, "I watch TV about 28 hours a week ... I spend about 45 minutes a day on homework".

Tyson reported that: "Right now I have no particular goal besides getting out of high school ... I have recently gotten serious about education".

Oban is in the college program. In response to a question on hindrances, he said: "I would have to hinder me. I make a decision not to allow others to tell me what to do".

Goal completion is the attainment of an expressed end-state. The process ends in success of some intentional goal.

For purposes of this study, I would argue that the goal-setting sequence would have to get to a stage where a goal is expressed before it could be considered as a goal. There must be goal specificity. Goals can be named or indicated in the life activities or shared stories given by the adolescents. The responses of the adolescents indicate a participation of the students in a goal-setting process. This narrative information includes the role of key players, challenges, and interacting episodes which influence the process. Some of the key players include a mother, father, or grandmother. Sometimes the presence of violence in the school or neighborhood makes the adolescent think about his future. A divorce or an observation about one's self or poor performance can become a sobering reality. A combination of factors about the school experience may gradually move the student to make decisions about his future.

In regards to social information, Counselor #3 said that: "White entering students have a wider range of information about things in general and are more prepared to do high school work than Black entering students". Pinnock's life shows that family income and socialization practices can provide the adolescent with a greater advantage in school transition and achievement.

Goal Movement in Urban Adolescent Life

Those adolescents who were interviewed shared accounts of their personal experiences. I reported some of these experiences earlier in the research. These experiences reflected what these students were going through during their educational "journey." Fason said it best when he reported, "I didn't have a purpose. I was in my freshman year at high school and still didn't have a clue about my future".

Fason did make it into the college program. Tyson, who was in the general program, said, "I have recently gotten serious about education. I was just getting by." Themos also reported his past condition: "I became lazy, I cut classes. I did not do well. . .my obstacle is that I doubt myself. I procrastinate. I can't seem to finish anything. I don't know why".

The account by the students in this chapter showed a trend of goal-setting phases. These phases or steps ranged from initial apathy and indifference to the actual setting of goals. Students were at different stages in their process of preparing for the future and becoming a success. Goal movement, when put into a sequence of activities, is reflected in these steps:

1. Uncertainty, unmotivated, undecided
2. Thinking, reflecting, evaluating one's situation
3. Deciding, choosing to act about a goal
4. Engaging in a goal effort, doing something
5. Creating a plan of action, a general goal pathway
6. Goal persistence, engaging in a series of actions
7. Goal completion—finishing high school, college acceptance, or gaining sought-after employment or training

It does not mean that each student systematically goes through each step. Pinnock, for example, came to high school after he had already thought about his future. He had already chosen his goal. He wanted to be an actor. Yet, he still had to make further effort to continue his planned studies. He had to work to make his goal an eventual reality. But most of the adolescents had to struggle or wrestle with coming to grips with their future, their academic performance, and their goals. They began to realize that their goals needed effort, planning, support, and encouragement (push) to make them happen.

Some of the students named a goal but were at a standstill, like Bordan, who was enrolled in the general studies program and undecided about a career goal. He reported:

> I feel I should never give up. I am somewhat motivated to get it together and better manage my time. I find it difficult to block out my time for study. . .I realize that I needed to do something about my future. I started to worry about what was going to happen to me later on.

Rhad, who was in grade 12 (general program) and still shaky about the future, said:

> I hope to get a degree at some point after high school … I watch a lot of TV, I eat too much candy, and my test-taking skills are not that great. I keep failing all the Regents. I failed five times.

Emil was in the 12th grade, and did not do well either, with his average of 69 in the general program. He said:

> I had to get a goal to get out of high school. I could not think about going to college because money was the problem. For my first two years in high school no one tried to help me. I did not try to see anyone either. I realized that I needed to study and pass or get kicked out. This woke me up.

The steps outlined represent a general series of experiences reflected in the study. All of the students interviewed went through some or all of these steps before a goal were reached. Some did not reach any goal. Most of the adolescents named a goal, but naming a goal does not create a goal without any accompanied goal effort (McClelland).

Some students responded to environmental conditions, family problems, episodic events, or poor reports from the school. Something happened to cause reflection or decision making. Some students needed provocative situations to move them to act in their own educational self-interest.

Some theorists (such as McCollom) state that movement from one stage or step to another is not smooth or continuous but episodic. Episodes and events trigger movement. Things happen in people's lives to move them to make an effort to overcome a particular state. Theorists also argue that each step or stage represents a distinct structure. That is, structure represents a group of distinct characteristics, features, or assumptions that describe what is occurring at that stage. Byzan, for example, went through the common emotions of despair that children experience when parents divorce. The same is true for victims of abuse or violence. The question of what hindrances may be present at each stage is very relevant to the particular adolescent. Even a lack of encouragement by others at home or school can become a hindrance.

Bargh and Gollwitzer point out that the environment can in many ways "control" goal-directed behavior. This control is exercised through impacting strategic goal routes the person may take. In other words there are "invisible" characteristics/factors in the environment that effectively hinder and limit individual movement of the person. The person may be subject to limitations in information provided by the social environment. Certain features of the environment can be intimidating to some. Byzan could not get past feelings of incompetence. He did not seek help. No one asked him about his goals in the school. Limitations could be reflected in the program the student has been assigned. Iane reported that he got used to his assigned general program and accepted it without any effort to move beyond that program.

In other cases, individuals may not be able to interpret activities in the environment that might be relevant to their goals. They may not be able to take advantage of what is available to them without help. Byzan could have benefited from a more informative program that could have reinforced his earlier medical goals. He could have found ways to demonstrate his academic ability.

There are other possible means in which environment can impact upon the goal-setting process. These can include the power of evaluation of educational policies and students, steering activities, and the power to distribute human and economic resources (Massey & Denton). The power of evaluation means that the decisions of others weigh heavily on credentializing and grading the effort and competence of another. The nature of the school itself is evaluative. The student is constantly being evaluated and assigned. The students reported both educational and environmental impacts upon their lives. Tyson said that when he was in the 5th grade a teacher called him "stupid" and he never got over it. As it turned out, he had eye problems that affected his reading. This was later corrected. William reported that "if you are doing poorly in school most counselors don't want to be bothered with you." Peterson said, "Unless you are a part of the college program counselors will not talk to you about college." Rhad reported, "If your homework was not current, the teacher would quietly fail you without notice." Eston said, "One teacher did not want to give me a handout in class because she said I might not even show up again". The evaluating teacher implied that Eston was unpredictable and would not get any better. He was not worth the assignment paper.

Two 9th graders, Pinnock and Conroy, who were honor students, had A averages in middle school, yet could not pass the test for the high school of their choice. Another 9th grader, Iane, thought he was signing up for legal courses in the public service program and found himself in the ROTC program that was associated with it. But he did not know. Iane was evaluated and directed by those in the school who were helping him "to decide."

Surrounding Conditions and Goal-Setting

The existential state means that the student has developed in a given social-psychological mind-set and experience near conceptions about the world. Social experience helps to inform adolescent social conceptions. The student has to launch his place in the world from an existential ambiguous platform, as the data has shown. In the case of many urban Black adolescents, the platform is one of academic dormancy and uncertainty. Students live in a world where structures and people are in opposition (Giddens). Rhad declared: "I don't like society. Blacks are treated bad...I need to be treated with respect". Monk said, "Society is rough. You have to stay positive to survive".

Byzan said that he had to make an effort to stay clear of drugs and violence in his neighborhood. Bordan said that he could not get a job in his area. Eston, Swan, and Monk reported that their mothers worked many hours in a nursing home.

The *thinking stage* indicates that students are beginning to sort things out. They are assessing reality. Emil said that: "it was during my sophomore year that I began to realize that I had to get my act together. Things were getting tougher out there economically."

Fason reported, "I grew up learning how to live without money. This made me think about purpose. I didn't have a purpose. I was in my freshman year in high school and still didn't have a clue about my future".

Decision making reflects statements indicating a decision is about to be made, has been made or needs to be made. Tyson said, "I have recently gotten serous about education. I was just getting by".

Goal naming states that certain goals or aspirations have been named, pointed out, wished for, or contemplated. Swan said, "I really want to be an engineer." Naming is different from goal specificity. Specificity occurs after the environmental field is surveyed and an informed decision has been made. Specificity follows personal investigation and evaluation but naming is an important step.

Project assignment and goal effort are indications that a particular goal is in serious pursuit. Some type of process has been asserted or initiated. It means that a goal delivery system has been envisioned and that a mental strategy is being formulated. For example, the student now goes to see his counselor not about schedules but about courses that are relevant to his goals. Themos went to summer school. He said, "Going to summer school made me serious because I didn't want to do it again." Themos began to see that doing poorly has its consequences.

A part of goal completion is the completion of some vital aspect of a given stage. This completion sets up the next stage in the sequence. Rhad reported, "I am struggling to maintain an 80–85 average. I am in the middle of my class of 400 students. I hope to get a degree at some point after high school." He said that nothing much happened in middle school, but: "when I came to the high school I had a long time interest in computers. Therefore, I took two semesters of computers, science, and math". His average was 85, and his science average was 80. Because Peterson followed through with his interest and grades, he was admitted to Brooklyn Technological College. He made computers a personal assignment. He went to see his counselors. They wanted him to focus on getting out of high school. He did this, but he also kept his focus on computers. In time he was able to move beyond the get out of high school syndrome and pursue his goal.

During motivational inertia and episodic awakening, it is common in mainstream society for a high level of interest and arousal to be present (Long). This is not necessarily the case for Black adolescents. The data has showed that for the Black adolescent, arousal can occur out of a sense of necessity, despair, desperation and tragic events. The core of the arousal may not be in the interest of learning. The adolescent may sense that he is in bad shape and others around him are in bad shape. So the adolescent strives to get on with it.

In the study, few students were enthusiastic about discussing their futures. The great sense of anticipation and success was not there. The students desired a good life but were not overly optimistic about the future. Rather, they seemed to have a feeling that they had to get past this phase. Tyson said, "My family made me "interested". They reminded me of how hard it is in the world. I am trying to get out of high school".

Academic Performance Curve Chart

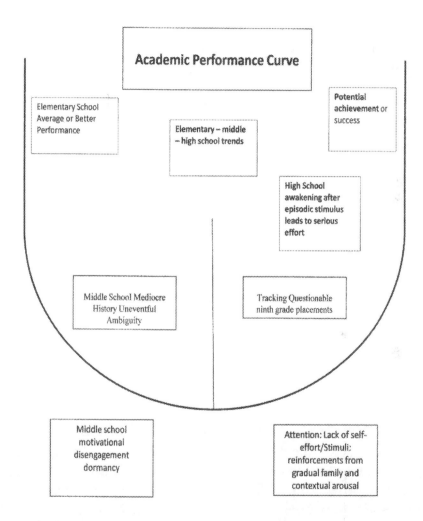

Note: the curve represents the experience of many Black urban males in the study. It is not generalized to all Black males. The curve includes those adolescents who become motivationally challenged overtime.

Adolescent Motivational Curve

William said:

Blacks are all messed up. They talk about themselves. They are going through too much in life. Yes rappers are messed up and they talk about themselves being messed up. In society you have to fight for success. . .you could get stressed out and smoke weed.

For the Black adolescent, effort is the breakthrough energy for overcoming contextual and personal challenges that hinder well-being and an academic mind-set. Effort is often launched from the matrix of dormancy and inactivity that has become an embedded routine. Incentives must be powerful and relevant in order to move the adolescent from ambiguity to reflection and decision-making. Each stage in the goal-setting process needs continual breakthrough effort, not just in a one-time step of decision making without follow-up. It is more than a leap of faith which can happen, but is rare. There must be a major effort until goal setting has become a routine activity seen in sub-steps. If this does not occur, the student will continue to suffer from contextual motivational inertia.

The Neighborhood and Well-Being

These are composite indicators of what people must contend with in order to achieve subjective well-being and success in life. They indicate the structure of social reality from an objective "scientific" perspective. If we look at the city neighborhoods involved in the study, county data indicate that in every major category there are challenges to overcome. Adolescents must cope with these challenges and set goals at the same time. But these challenges seem "natural" to the environment it could lead to quiet acquiescence.

Eston, who has lived in the area of the study all of his life, said, "I grew up inside the house. There were too many gangs outside". Rhad reported that in his neighborhood, "There are drug dealers, fights, cops and police. The police don't have any effect on the drug pushers. . . I don't do anything stupid so I won't incite the police".

It is a reminder that critical (effective) stimuli and ongoing episodic events in the environment play a role in shaping the response character of urban adolescents. In terms of the study context, up to 42 percent of the immediate neighborhoods were in poverty. The official unemployment rate was over 9 percent. There were over 5,341 arrests for drug-related crimes and over 7,000 rapes annually. There were many low-performing public schools in terms of state reading and math scores. There were gang wars and documented complaints about wandering bands of youth in the streets. There were numerous recorded calls to the city about poor sanitary conditions. These conditions existed within 9 square miles.

In regards to decision making, students must resolve to focus upon schoolwork and avoid police clashes while struggling with low family income. In other words, despite the reality of the social conditions, a decision must be made to make a committed effort to succeed and achieve in the context of an oppressive urban environment. The study shows that many of the adolescents were concerned about success and well-being. Oban, who was in the college honors program, stated that: "It is important to me to be something. Success is to be all you can be".

It is in the context of an oppressive environment that references to hip-hop music became important. Some adolescents reported that they like hip-hop music. This was emphasized to the research assistant. The adolescents felt that there was still some public suspicion about the legitimacy and acceptance of the hip-hop culture and message. This is why William reported that "hip-hop provokes Whites". William probably suspected that I might also be offended because I was outside of his age group and culture (at least for this part of the interview.) Those who seemed better off would be the targets of criticism.

William did not like his neighborhood. He didn't feel that society was fair and when he went to the high school he decided to be a laid-back student. He said he wanted to be himself. William stated, "I am interested in being an electrician and to run a supply house before I am 30, but I hate math and electronic engineering." It appeared that William had lost the will to bounce back. For a long while William didn't want to make a real effort to succeed. He said, "be yourself.

Don't try to take on the world before your time." William, however, did say that "young men should stay in school even if you didn't get anything." William did not sound like he was excited about his future. It was, however, his interest in hip-hop that encouraged me to arrange future interviews for him with the research assistant.

Yeah I Can Relate to It: Hip-Hop and the Black Urban Experience

I did not realize the significance of hip-hop in the lives of Black adolescents initially in the study. The responses to questions about their views of society were expected. Society was unfair, condescending, and biased. But the adolescents didn't seem all that concerned about society. There was little indication of any strong feeling about the unfairness of society. Their answers to questions about society were cut and dry. It was almost assumed that this is the way it is. The adolescent generally reported that with hard work you could overcome the barriers of society and its tendencies towards injustice and ruthless competition. Eston said, in regards to personal feelings about society, "it will neither help you or stop you from doing what you want. You have to put your own mind to what you want. You have to do with what you have". But when a few of the adolescents mentioned a few things about hip-hop music I scheduled additional interviews for them to discuss hip-hop with the research assistant. The adolescents gladly discussed questions about their love for hip-hop. I discovered that the adolescents were letting the hip-hop artists or rappers do the talking for them. The rappers could see all of the contradictions and exploitations of society and turned their insights into a public forum through the music (Rose. Dawson says that the Black community becomes a "counter public" in its social perspectives. Dawson says that ideology needs a public sphere of debate and discussion. In the medium of hip-hop music, a public sphere has been created that has become the voices of those who might not say much but who do think. This is a form of what is called oppositional culture. The students were not oppositional in speech or behavior, but they listened to those who were.

Some adolescents reported that they liked the messages of the rappers. They could relate to them because they liked the lyrics. The lyrics reflect reality—their reality. Their stories were being told by those who had gone through the same things, usually in the urban context. The research assistant concentrated on why some of the adolescents liked hip-hop music and why it was so popular at parties that they attended. Five students made strong points about the role of hip-hop. There were three main themes that stood out in the interviews.

Balwin stated that:

Music reinforces the sound and struggles of the street. DMX shares his struggles. The good part is that the music deals with reality. It helps remind you of the idea that you must finally come to grips with what is out there, that you ain't got no choice. The music talks about violence, being caged in your home, your neighborhood as a grave, feeling twisted, sometimes things being out of control, girls, set parties, relationships, and hard life in the world. Music tells you about the real deal in the world and what a fight there is dealing with prison, the hustle, the addicted, drugs, and the evil in society.

William said:

hip-hop makes Whites angry. Blacks are not liked because they are too outspoken and hip-hop makes it worse. If there were more rappers, things could be helped to get better. Rappers speak about how the world deals with us. For example, Police Enemy, Jay-Z, 50 cents and PCB.

Byzan said, "I think music has the biggest affect (on my peers) especially hip-hop".

Monk said:

I like hip-hop and reggae. I listen to different artists like Jay-Z and DMX. . . . Society is rough. You have to stay positive to survive. . .sometimes at a party people make slurs about different things like knocking yourself out to please other people and doing your own thing. . . . Society is a bad place and you don't need others telling you what to do.

The theme of reality was the most prominent. Monk said: "I like their lyrics. They 'spit' some real shi@!#. Yeah, I can relate to it. It's real, it's about some real life. I like that". Fason reported, "My favorite song is 'Kiss Your Ass Goodbye 50 Cent' (by Style Speaks). He is talking about taking 50 Cent out both literally and figuratively in that song". Monk said that the song he likes is "Put Your Hands Up" by ESAP.

The second most popular theme was business and success. This was very important to the adolescents. Byzan said that his favorite hip-hop artist was Jay'Z. He stated:

I like the fact that he is a businessman and his lyrics. Jay'Z is an entrepreneur. He does rap, a record label, clothes, he does a lot. He's just business. I am intrigued by him. He's into everything. He's making money.

Tyson reported that he likes 50 Cent. He said, "I like his lyrics, like 'Hustlers Ambition'—telling you how to make it. There is a song that talks about life and being shot and how it is an interesting life. I like that one." He said, "I like Jay'Z. He is intelligent. He's making smart moves; creating monopolies, buying teams, bottles, drinks, he's intelligent. It is smart, yeah, they're making money".

The third theme that stood out was about growing up. Bordan said,

The songs I like the best would be from Blue Print's #11 'Mama Loves Me.' It reminds me of life growing up. I can identify with that. Yeah, that is why I like it, I identify with life and with my mother.

Tyson said that he

identifies with the song "Mama Loves Me" because it shows how the artist grew up. He made it. He grew up in poverty and made it. I like that. He also tells you not to do it (the drugs) and to stay out of the drug game. We listen to hip-hop at parties and other music that we dance to, like R&B. The greatest rapper is Big E Smalls (same as the Notorious BIG). His lyrics were out there. And he was just cool and laid-back. I go to parties for the girls and the music. I am not a wall hugger. I don't stand around the walls and look. No I dance!

The results of the hip-hop interviews indicate again that the adolescents were interested in dealing with social reality. It was obviously of great concern to them and their well-being. Being successful is a continuing theme in the study. The students were in a sense applauding those who made it in society despite the obstacles. This is a major achievement. Even Jay Z was admired for his worldly intelligence and smart economic moves. It is also an admirable way to become successful, attain well-being, and not necessarily rely upon the social institutions that represent contextual struggles, unfairness, and negative evaluation.

During the high school interviews, the students shared information about being poor. They talked about struggling mothers working in hospitals and nursing homes. The students talked about violent street conditions, bad police encounters, and the difficulty in finding jobs. Official unemployment reports showed poverty or near-poverty conditions in the test neighborhood. The experience of growing up was something they did not forget. The student's reflections on the conditions of growing up helped them to appreciate their hard-working mothers and the value of pursuing the goal of well-being and success. Their mothers worked in order to overcome economic and social obstacles. They wanted to move beyond survival if they could.

From Goal Hindrances to Goal Strategies

The lack of goals is reflected in the lack of interest in schooling. This becomes a hindrance. If the student is unsure about goals he may be uncertain about learning and developing strategies for any future goals. Bargh and Gollwitzer state that goals are less likely to be achieved without an immediate strategy in place. They maintain that questions about hindrances and control do not come into play until after the strategy is in place. I do not agree with this argument. Hindrances can be at work, affecting the student's interest, enthusiasm, and motivation to achieve. Strategy acts as a means to increase commitment and activity. Strategy appears as a step in the goal-setting sequence in this study. Goal setting is defined on the basis of steps that occur or develop in time. It is a sequence that selects, names, and commits the person to an assigned task, as confirmed by strategy and effort. Strategy is needed, but a decision-making process must be activated first.

Byzan, who is a fairly good student in the general studies program but uncertain about the future, said that: "getting caught up in gang participation, getting a girl pregnant, cutting classes, hanging out after school, failing to avoid drugs and violence" would hinder him because of what he has already seen in the neighborhood.

Bordan reported that "trouble with the law" would be an obstacle to him because he had already had a run in with the police at a local park for playing until dusk one evening.

Monk and Rhad reported that "fear of death," through violence, drugs, bad friends, and violent people would serve as hindrances to attaining goals.

Tyson and Swan said that not making any effort and laziness would cause them not to attain their goals. Peterson reported that "I need money for school." Themos was very angry at himself for his poor school record. (His GPA was 69 in the general program). Themos reported earlier that: "I doubt myself, I procrastinate, I can't seem to finish anything".

These responses can be summarized as (a) environmental turbulences and vices; (b) personal weaknesses, such as poor study habits, failures in school, a lack of personal discipline; and (c) economic challenges.

There is another important question that is related to goal setting: Is the desire for well-being and success a goal? Success, we know, is important to adolescents. But success and well-being are just ideas until motive, effort, and strategy come together around a specific goal. But motive must come first; specificity comes afterward. The desire for success and well-being can be the motive for goal setting and achievement. Well-being and success are so general the person's development could lag a long time without producing any results.

Since effort is an important component of goal-setting motivation, it must be incorporated and encouraged. Effort must be rewarded. Hindrances must be minimized if possible. There must be feedback about efforts that are made. But in most places achievement is rewarded over effort (Long). You cannot achieve anything without effort and students need to be encouraged to make an effort. Yet achievement is always seen in isolation when rewards are dispensed. Rewards must be linked to learning and effort, not just competence and ability. Many students are slower learners or must overcome long-term handicaps. For contextually challenged students, the effort stage is an achievement stage. This is important because some researchers argue (McCaslin and DiMarino-Linnen) that proactive humans have a natural inclination to do something about their restrictive environments. This is easier said than done in some environments. This is an awesome task for adolescents to take on. But self action and taking charge of one's life can be encouraged. This is why most of the parents in the study encouraged the student to take education seriously by doing well in school. Barry, an average student, said, "My mother encourages me in my educational life." Swan reported that his mother and grandmother encouraged him, despite his laziness.

During the study, adolescents gave various responses to questions about hindrances, goal setting, and success. The task was to examine the responses in order to better understand the social realities that move the life process of adolescents in a given direction. No one factor would block the academic and social progress of such a large urban group. A combination of environmental factors works to distract and deter students from improving their performance.

After examining student self-reports, it appears that the question of hindrances is really a part of the students' contextual lives. All the things that were mentioned were in fact honest replies, but the greater picture involves the entire trajectory of adolescent life. The challenges of hindrances are really a composite factor. Hindrances involve the total succession of events that impact upon the life of the person.

The life pattern trajectory includes contextual stress and economic pressure upon marginalized families. Many adverse factors working together produce hindrances. They affect student focus, interest, and sense of confidence in the academic process. Students became disengaged from intellectual pursuits because their competing life patterns were incompatible with academic achievement. School tracking structures and culture peer networks has helped to normalize a reactionary life for the adolescents. This creates a trajectory which propels the adolescent into ongoing ambiguity and motivational dip (loss of interest). The momentum of the trajectory can be changed if there are relevant environmental stimuli. Stimuli like community role models and relevant information on future options can encourage a desire for better behavioral regulation and self-discipline. Goals provide a reason to exercise personal initiative and autonomy. Goals can become the cornerstone of subjective well-being. Goals follow self-interest. Goals clarify what is to be done in order to create a higher level of well-being (Oishi).

I would argue that successful adolescents have moved into an academic flow pattern or a new trajectory. A cohesive flow must be developed, not just isolated efforts of improvement. Academic flow and a momentum is what Black adolescents didn't seem to have. Flow is a continuous related involvement and preoccupation with an activity. The motivated life includes structure, routine and a particular style. The person navigates challenges that arise with greater ease and courage. Black adolescents in the study had experienced numerous episodic interruptions that made it difficult for them to get into a routine of study and progress. Themos suffered from procrastination. Swan admitted he was lazy. Tyson didn't make any effort and Rhad bragged that he had failed his math Regents five times. (Although I would argue that his bragging covers up a fear of failure and embarrassment by projecting an "I don't really care" attitude.) At the same time that some of the adolescents were doing poorly in school they were spending a lot of time watching TV and not on additional study. Rhad said that most of the other students he knew failed their math Regents also. I would say, "So what!" This provides a cushion and an excuse for failure.

Csikszentmihalyi and Rathunde claim that when experiences are not rewarding, people stop the activity or disengage themselves from it. Many adolescents apparently disengage themselves from meaningful school activities after poor performances. Some theorists argue for example, Gollwitzer that in order to perform the task at hand the mind activates a certain process that creates a way to perform the task (problem-solving mind-set). But when a new task is given, the previous mind-set has difficulty changing over to a different way of functioning. The mental pattern of Brain circuitry has already set in. The mind needs a new orientation. It needs to reflect upon a wider field of information as input. If the adolescent is experiencing a state of dormancy and intellectual disengagement in middle school, a mental changeover is needed in order for him to function successfully in high school. This changeover is not easy to accomplish. This means that the first step in the goal-setting process (awakening) is critical. The student has to move beyond past hindrances with new thinking and mental strategy. This process will be discussed in detail in the next chapter.

A different mind-set is needed in the planning and execution of goal-directed academic behavior. A new openness and deliberation for action is needed for the intellectually dormant person. The inert mind-set requires a lot of stimulating engagement. In this case, rewarding reinforcements are needed to encourage students to move to another step in goal activity. This requires some kind of cognitive readjustment.

In regards to society and hindrances, many adolescents reported clashes with the police and some form of discrimination. Rhad said he didn't like society because of how Blacks are treated. Bordan has faced racism, especially in employment. Williams said, "you have to fight for fairness," and Themos reported that "it is hard to do anything. If you play football, the cops come and take the football. . . If you play basketball, the cops come and take the basketball." Monk said, "I have been harassed by Black and White police alike." Balwin said, "I stay away from cops." Oban states that he was cuffed and arrested for disorderly conduct because he bad-mouthed a cop who was on his back. The question is raised about what these adolescents do to deal with apparent existential stress or social anxiety. The adolescents dealt with some stress through music and sometimes parties. Some students watched a lot of TV, some hung out with friends. But others downplayed hanging out. Bordan said: "Yes I go out with my friends in the city but I don't hang out in the streets." He wanted the interviewer to know that he was not a street person. He was protecting his image.

Leary and Kowalski point out that people who face society with apprehension will tend to withdraw and become socially inhibited. By withdrawing individuals may escape the anxiety-producing environment; they participate less in the threatening social context and find another domain of social activity. People tend to go where feelings of discomfort and well-being can be dealt with in a positive and free manner. The period of adolescence is one of life, energy, vigor, and felt freedom. Adolescents need a changeover activity as an act of liberation and relief. This happens, in part, through entertainment, sports, and parties. These events can be distracting if over done. In the global world context people need to maintain motivating, focused and disciplined life-styles.

The Central Question: Motivation
Success and Goal-Setting

Most of the Black adolescents in the study shared that they engaged in idealistic notions about social success and well-being. Their conceptions were reflected in their conversations, but not in their academic habits (life-styles). Many adolescents who said they wanted to go to college spent little time on homework. Byzan, who spent 45 minutes a day on homework, said, "The homework is easy." But Byzan was enrolled in the general, non challenging program. Tyson, who had a 77 average in the general program, said, "Success is making a goal for yourself and working to the fullest extent to make it possible." Yet Tyson had no goal except to get out of high school. He watched TV 7 hours a day and did 1/2 hour to 1 hour of homework daily. The students, therefore, needed to make a connection between abstract personal success and academic success. They needed to engage in a goal process that would translate their desire for increased well-being into a series of steps leading to specific goal attainment.

The study did not anticipate an involved process in the enactment of goal-setting activity and achievement. This is more than plugging in a definition of goal setting and stating the results. The study showed that for most of the adolescents, regardless of goal naming, there was little to show in regards to actual goal striving. Goal setting results in a committed pattern of a prolonged process and some lifestyle adjustments. Most of the adolescents who had experienced a personal awakening that followed a period of "motivational dip" did start to make decisions about their future. Those who were still uncertain about their interest, future, or needs did not seriously participate in a goal-setting process. It could be that they thought they had time to plan later. But as time passed they realized in this (global) study their future life could get lost.

The answer to the question of whether or not Black adolescents set goals is intricate. Many adolescents in the study slowly began to become futuristic in their thinking. In their high school career (or before) some of them had been stimulated to reflect on their academic performance. The end result of this reflection was a reorientation towards taking life and schooling more seriously. There was less emphasis on teacher relations and other matters. Composite factors of parental advice and environmental circumstances caused some students to reassess their school performance and personal direction.

Motivational literature has emphasized achievement motivation in restricted terms. Most motivation scholars define achievement chiefly in terms of academic and school success (Covington). The need to achieve was a prominent theme in the literature. Academic achievement involves the process of outperforming others and showing one's ability status for mainstream society. Success is defined by many mainstream researchers as the need for mastery and in testing results. Eccles and Wigfield state that in the past, achievement performance and choice was linked to high individual expectancy, academic values and beliefs. But recent motivation theory now links these components to a broader spectrum of psychological and social/cultural determinants. Students must now be psychologically linked to the academic and global world in order to approach the demands of a testing, evaluative society. These determinants inform how motivation is going to be played out in the real context of the institutional – social arena.

According to the study, many of these adolescents did not view school achievement as a means to success. The school almost seemed as an obstacle to getting to success and the challenges of life. School was something imposed by society. The students needed school because society set the standard. Some adolescents reported that the school did not deal with reality, (while hip-hop did). In time some students realized that life was too difficult to succeed without school preparation. Monk said, "The student ought to be prepared for what you have to face out there". Tyson, who was an average student, said, "My family reminds me of how hard it is in the world". Themos had a poor school record but reported that "to be successful you must go to school". In terms of this study, I would argue that research cannot be accurate if it attempts to evaluate motivation without including contextual factors and the adolescent's understanding of success. Motivation for some adolescents is not about outperforming others and showing ones' ability status. It is more about being oneself and using success to achieve a higher level of well-being. Many African American adolescents value their well-being, respect, and economic success beyond an abstract admiration for school. Goal setting involves ongoing self and environmental evaluation. Goal setting answers the question of how personal and school information fits into the adolescent's need-world and well-being.

In this study, many adolescents sought the general goal of success and well-being, not necessarily academic excellence. The academic goal of performing well in school occurred when there was a strong motive or incentive to accomplish a success goal. This incentive usually came from parents in combination with episodic events.

Coach Them On: Family Support for Education

"My mother gives me personal encouragement. A lot of people don't do well and they may not have that person to coach them on," said Swan. Monk said, "My mother is my best supporter regarding education. She is my coach." This was a constant theme throughout the interviews. Mothers in the study often acted as education coaches.

The adolescents were encouraged by most parents despite the fact that most of these families lacked the expertise to provide hands-on academic information. Parents did not help with homework or provide more detailed support beyond encouragement. Not one student reported any practical help from parents. Their help was to "push" the student in taking education seriously. However, in time, most students benefited from parental encouragement. Sometimes it was too late to affect their grade averages. There were a few meaningful contacts with other college-age relatives or parents. Many of the parents in the study worked in low-paying jobs in local hospitals. In other words, there were few indications in the study that these students had the kind of connections that could raise their personal interest or goals beyond home encouragement. The students were limited in their interactions with other successful students actually in college or in other careers.

Black parents want to be involved with their students. The parents' limited availability restricted the amount of support they could offer. Many parents were not even home when the student was doing a small amount of homework. Most students did less than an hour's worth of homework per night while carrying six or seven subjects. Parents who are home more often can make the difference between the student's excelling or just getting by. When the parent has more time to give it can make a difference in motivational intensity

The study shows that family support is a major source of encouragement for Black adolescents. According to this study, even in one-parent households the parent was a strong supporter of school attendance, better grades, less street involvement, and consistent homework for future achievement. This support also came from the extended family.

Rhad said, "My brother-in-law told me about different colleges." Monk reported, "my mother and cousin support me. My father encouraged me even when my parents separated. My father said, go to school and pass. Education is important." Some students who were hanging in academic limbo were encouraged. Swan said, "My mother and grandmother encouraged me. My mother talks to me about cutting classes and school things". Even in the pilot study, Barry reported, "My mother encouraged me, but I don't have a real closeness to my mother because she works a lot. My father is dead. My uncle (mother's brother) encourages me".

Mr. Blan, student affairs director, said,

First, many students have to act as parents and sitters for their siblings while the parents are at work. So they go right home from school. Secondly, a few students have part time jobs and they need the money. They must choose between the benefits of school activities or working. Thirdly, there are many students who just don't have an interest or see the relevance of these activities. It is this group of students that desire to leave the premises as soon as school is over, that is the greatest concern"

What Mr. Blan is reporting is that the students need encouragement but also more connection with the school as a support system in itself. A better connection might help the adolescent to perform better despite the domestic challenges at home. Parents are also trying to cope with life.

Counselor #3 reported that:

The frustration level among many parents is high. We have parents' meeting night and many parents are on edge because of general life pressures and the pressure of poor-performing children. One night there was a meeting with parents. One mother became enraged and began to yell and curse at me while the other parents were sitting in the room. Her son was not doing well in school. The real shocker was that the other parents said nothing to her. I was absolutely appalled, not at the mother who was yelling, but at the passive indifference of those who sat around and did not help. . .The parents are busy attempting to survive. They need to get focused. Frustrated parents don't always know what the student is doing or not doing. When the parents or students finally come in to see the counselor they come without making appointments. Sometimes appointments are non-existent. . . Parental cooperation is necessary. Constant contact is needed with the school not just when the light bulb goes off and the parent and student wake up. Then there is nothing left for the student but the marines or the armed forces.

Counselor #2 said that:

Parents must be sent for when poor grades are reported for their child. If we do not send for them we might never see them. We are well aware, however, that many parents work one to two jobs to make ends meet. Many of them are overwhelmed.

These statements by students and counselors serve to reinforce the need to find a way to set goals and achieve in society rather than repeat the cycle of anger and/or failure. There is a great need to rise above a marginalized life and begin to live.

Parents At Work

Oban reported:

My mother works various hours as a cook at a nearby hospital and I may not see her. I go home and go right to sleep. The next day if I don't have the homework to turn in, the teacher just looks at you and says nothing.

Some students reported the occupation of their parent(s). Many of them were employed in either hospitals, nursing homes, or other low-wage jobs. Those parents who worked in nursing homes or hospitals served as aides. Figure #3 reflects some parental occupations.

Parents at Work

Student	GPA	Program	Parent's Occupation
Bordan	80	General	Hospital (Mother)

Eston	65	General	Hospital (Mother)
Emil	69	General	Hospital (both parents)
Monk	78	General	Nursing home (Mother & cousin)
Swan	77	General	Nursing home (Mother)
Peterson	80	College	Hospital (Mother)
Oban	70	College	Hospital (Mother)
Carlin	70	General	Janitor (Father)
William	68	General	Store clerk (Mother)
Fason	80	College	Security guard (Mother)

Parents At Work

This chapter discussed and analyzed the relevant aspects of adolescent goal setting. School, family, and environmental factors were analyzed to examine conditions under which these students struggled to come to grips with their future. The struggle included reflecting upon the current state of the adolescent, and making decisions, effort, and lifestyle changes in a continuing goal-setting process. This process included contextual concerns, valuing education, social concerns, and well-being while facing an uncertain future.

After having examined these factors, the next challenge is to see how we can use that information to follow-up with intervention strategies, additional research, and theory building. The main themes described in the research will be discussed in the next chapter.

What Do They Want: Adolescents in the Study

In summation, many students had similar desires or needs. Certain needs were more pronounced than others. These are the desires that seemed to have had a great deal of consistency in some students (as previously reported in the study):

They want a responsive school environment (teachers who act concerned).

Eston said: "The teachers were aloof. They didn't really get involved [with student concerns]." Byzan stated that: "No, no one asked me anything [about my goals]. I just went to class or scheduled meetings with my advisor." Bordan said that by grade 10 "[in the general program] only three teachers acted like they had an interest in me."

They want an education that is relevant to the real world.

Swan, who was in his last year, emphasized that: "I get more good advice from home than I do at school. The main focus of the school is to help you graduate and get a diploma. That's it!" Monk said: "But what I think is really unfair about society is that it does not prepare you for what you have to face out there. We are not programmed to deal with society." Baldwin stated: "The good part is that the music deals with reality."

They want meaningful, relevant counseling that deals with future goals and not just scheduling set school agendas.

William stated that: "Counselors give you good advice when they have time. I feel that they are there to carry out a job and do not necessarily have a personal interest in the student. In other words, they are there for show." Byzan said, "I drop into my counselor's office once a week for a few hot minutes just to say bye." Rhad reported, "My counselors gave me a plan. They said you must pass all of your courses or you will only be allowed to take basic stuff—nothing extra was offered." Tyson said: "I go in, check grades and things like that. They only call me for scheduling matters or if there seems to be a communication problem at home." Swan stated, "No, I didn't think to ask how to move on my career and she (counselor) didn't ask me." Peterson said, "Counselors don't get deep into personal goals, but if and only if you are from a certain program like the college program will they talk to you about college admission."

They want economic stability and opportunities.

Emil said that, in the past, "We really suffered. We were bad off for a great while. We could not pay the rent. We had to move out of our apartment." William complained, "Right now I am not successful. I don't have ten dollars in my pocket." Themos reported: "My father just went back to work after six months being unemployed." Swan said: "I don't have a job now. I am trying to get one." Bordan reported: "I face a lot of racism, especially in employment." Eston pledged that: "My mom is a nurse's aide and is constantly working. I have been trying to get a job. I will take any kind of job."

They want to live in a supportive, nonviolent, nonconfrontational environment.

Peterson stated:

The people who move into my neighborhood are worse than those who move out. It is noisy late at night with guns and fights. This is hard when you have to go to school the next day. It puts you in a state of imbalance and uneasy concern.

Themos reported: "I don't like my neighborhood. It is hard to do anything." Themos referred to aggressive police, parents who don't trust their children's friends, and crime in the neighborhood.

They want respect.

Bordan said that:

The way people look at you in a condescending way. They look down on you and I would feel better if people did not look down on me when I am in the public walking down the street. I want to be respected.

Eston reported that: "I don't want to learn just to be learning. I want to learn in order to be somebody." Emil shared in the interview that: "I like being in style. I like the way I look and fit in with the crowd. People look at you differently."

They want success, well-being, and autonomy.

Fason, who was already in the college program, was glad when the teacher told him, "You can do better. I can be a successful student." Monk reported that: "Success is the result of hard work. Don't wait upon others to help you who may have no interest in you." William, who was an average student, said that: "Success is not letting anyone interfere with your goals."

The Struggle Towards the Motivated Life
Arriving at a State of Mindfulness

Adolescent School Engagement
Lack of "Institutional Push"
Low level commitment to learning
Line Academic Excitement
Non-provocative Environment
Undeveloped learning habits

Mindfulness Reflection — Coming to Grips with self
Coming to increased awareness
Activation: Episodic—Progressive—Gradual

Taking Charge of Self
Deciding, Goal Naming
Selected Strategy – Goal Pathway

Processing
Active goal pursuit
Action Follow-Up – Information Gathering
Personal Project Assignment – Self Imposed
Goal Effort -- Consistency

The Motivated Life
Goal Persistence: Lifestyle Adjustments
Achievement—Realization

CHAPTER 6
THE NEW PARADIGM OF THINKING, LEARNING AND LIVING

The purpose of this chapter is to deal with the insights of recent brain research and their implications for adolescent and adult intellectual development. This can lead to a more competent motivated life. In short, recent brain research has shown that the brain can, when actively engaged, (in thinking, effort and attention) develop itself. This chapter will link my study with recent research findings.

Let us begin with a brief summary of the study results and move into the findings of recent bran research. My study has shown that:

There was often a strong sense of academic ambiguity and uncertainty among students. There was also a weak sense of time and urgency. A significant lack of effort or push towards envisioned goals was present. The concentration level was weak in many students in the study. The adolescents generally did not have a strong focus or adequate means of coping with environmental challenges. Coming to grips with future goals and related preparation seemed to involve a long gradual process.

Many of those in the study were engaged in a slow process of finding themselves, success and ultimate well-being. One major aspect present in the vague pursuit for relevant education and viable goals was the lack of a pre-planned strategy and a clear sense of direction. Adequate support by interested others was also needed. Many of those who did receive support and encouragement obtained it from their families and in some cases teachers. A major factor in on-going academic failure appeared to be the lack of timely effort and response to move the student beyond the stigma of poor past performances. Some students seemed to be disoriented. Taking corrective measures was a project in itself. Taking the initiative to get beyond their present state was a major hurdle for many struggling adolescents. This involved reflecting, deciding and acting to set goals and engage in self-regulation for a motivated life.

This academic process involved factors such as arousal of emotional-mental fortitude and thinking through challenges. The goal-setting process involved establishing new thinking patterns and behavioral tendencies that could create goal pathways. In other words a whole new way of focusing (attending) needed to begin to condition the student for a motivated life style. Students should be encouraged to engage in intentional mental effort and focus directly upon meaningful objects of study. Students should avoid engaging in detached (surface) study and inquiry. This depth of focus can produce major results. Often a lack of familiarity gives the false impression that something is difficult when it may not be the case. Poor performance can result from low level engagement and a high level of fear and intimidation. Students who have experienced poor academic performances in the past can rise above previous results that indicated their mental capacities seemed to be restricted. It was rare that someone said to a struggling student "You can do it." Students need to know that they don't have to accept deterministic notions of fixed ability levels and limited intelligence. With the needed combination of effort, specific attention and support the student can increase his/her cognitive levels through greater use of intentional brain activity. Students can avoid the frustration of believing their assessed ability levels cannot rise. Recent research has shown that past experiences and cultural perspectives tend to become a part of individual mental networks. The brain then uses the same circuitry already set up in the mind (Wexler). Information processing, thinking, remembering, and feeling, this means that mind structures itself to limited perspectives and patterns of thought. Past negative social experiences and poor performance are incorporated in mental thought patterns. These patterns are difficult to change.

What Effort Will Do

Nisbet and Pervin related effort and attention to a social context. They argue that attention is an awakening experience that occurs in the environment. Attention acts to manipulate or accommodate something in the related world. Involved attention devises new modes of behavioral responses. Selective attention can eventually change behavior. Attention is a mental attitude and intention to actively process outside stimuli. Deliberate attention requires hard work and effort. When a habit of attention is developed, processing information in a particular domain becomes easier. John Taylor states that attention is the gateway to consciousness. It helps to unify consciousness. Habit involves repeated attention given to a particular object/subject. Habit reinforces thinking, understanding and learning. It helps to off-set and moves beyond mental dormancy and idle brain capacity. (This will be discussed in more detail.) Developing habits of attention involves ongoing effort and anticipated rewards

The level of effort (perseverance) is an index of motivation. It also incorporates a larger set of personal and social governing factors. These factors include: personal skills, felt competence, emotional state, social reinforcement, personal knowledge structures, feedback, past experiences, proper diet, and environmental opportunities. This is why personal striving is seen holistically as the motivated life.

Sometimes we assume that others are more intelligent than we are because they seem to know the subjects better. But, mental investment pays off. When you study and learn more in general you have more to bring to the table of understanding. You have more to work with. It makes problem solving in new areas (domains) easier for you. This is often why challenging material is often shut down quickly. In our minds we immediately recognize our apparent limitations. We fail to think through the possible rewards of our efforts, our values, and our future.

Intentions wane and die out without effort. This effort is necessary because of the boundary or distance between self and the environment. Frederick Perls who was a gestalt researcher stated that there is a psychological distance between the thoughts of the individual and the environment. When the individual begins to attend to some environmental stimulus that boundary begins to weaken and disappear. The environment can appear as a threat. Therefore, the individual needs to resist repressing his or herself (in effort) and focus upon relevant aspects of the environment. This must be done in order to successfully negotiate the objects of interest and bring them into the sphere of one's personal understanding. It is called psychological alignment. This, of course, depends upon subjective valuing (choices), openness and self control. It is an act of the responsible self.

The mind needs to have access and linkage to familiar aspects of a subject. This familiarity softens individual resistance to accept challenge. The student is gradually introduced to various perspectives of a subject to encourage continuance of inquiry and mental processing. It also helps the student to choose a style of learning and approach to a subject that perfects learning ("how to learn"). A comfortable pattern of engagement can be developed without making a permanent commitment to an uncertain goal.

From Effort to Cognition

Since effort is a summary term for many related activities; these activities must work together to make effort meaningful. Effort mediates other activities such as attention, information processing, sustained interest, information seeking and decision -making. Both attention and effort involves a cognition control of mental processes. The thinking process connects a perceived subject as a stimulus with encoded memory. This encoding is a form of a modified mental template. In other words, as the object is attended to, it is encoded so that it can be recalled or retrieved at another time from human memory. The retrieval is based upon some mental representation in memory. A template type mental image is coded so that it can be internally recognized by the individual for future processing. This is why learning helps more learning to occur. Students are able to recognize and better able to understand information that is already familiar to them. They are able to retain something about a particular subject or object.

The mind must act to reconstruct, infer, transfer and retrieve the encoded information for activated use. Concept mastery, images and ideas become easier to learn with added sequences of attended excitory (stimulating) signals. These sequences form mental circuits or patterns within each particular subject domain. The brain may also cross reference itself by sharing information across connected areas in the brain. Signals and stimuli provoke processing and recall. Each time similar information is processed the circuitry or connecting routes of brain neurons (connected nerve cells) get stronger (Leek). The process gets faster and easier to understand. This body of knowledge is categorized as cognitive biology, biological psychology or cognitive neuroscience. But most of these headings refer simply to brain activity and human behavior. They are related to the recent research interest and discoveries about brain plasticity. This will be discussed later.

This subject is very important to the study on adolescent motivation. Recent information on brain research reinforces my argument that with more specific effort in various academic domains students with even average intelligence can in fact excel. The old theory that intelligence is fixed or determined genetically at birth is not only outdated, but misleading. It is too deterministic and leads to the social-psychological position that Black students cannot do better. That is Black students cannot exceed the level of their assigned (measured) intelligence quotient based upon psychological testing. Much of the celebrated intelligence gap reports can, I argue be attributed to an attention and processing gap in the cognitive life of Black students. Those who concentrate more learn more. This does not include students with major drug histories or major sickness. However some of these students may also benefit from increased attention-effort processing. One of the IQ tests called the Sternberg Triachic model is made up of three parts. These parts are the analytic, creative and practical. The analytic part is particularly attention-processing dependant. This part in itself can distort testing results.

Student test taking attitudes and dispositions in a school setting can also skew results.

Since brain activity is a psychological-biological response to the environment that is amplified through attention, and transmission of information. Mental blocks or Jammes are forms of mental inertia resulting from brain under use. The person's mind ends up "stuck" in one mode because of lack of thinking and mental engagement. The individual at some point, however, should be able to break through mental disengagement and environmental turn offs through mindfulness, concentration, attention and reflection. Fighting distortions, fear and dormancy is just another bridge the under achieving adolescent must cross. Over involvement in some activities or negative associations in the urban culture can cause adolescents to confine their thinking to restricted domains that are not productive. Repeated experiences can affect brain structure. In this context if an executive attention network is in place it will deepen the awareness of the brain (canterior cingulated). This network includes receptivity, self observation and reflexivity (Siegel). In addition to brain activity, genetic activity also informs the level of brain performance. There are environmental dependent genes that respond to the environment and other genes as well. This affects gene expression as a consequence of environmental interaction and gene networking. (King, et al., Jensen, Nisbett, Watson)

Cognitive Plasticity: Brains Can Get Better

Recent bio-cognitive research as centered upon the increased capacity of the brain to improve its ability to create and transmit new neurotic (brain cell) connections and networks. This is called brain plasticity. The brain has many synapses or connections with other brain cells (neurons). Some may disappear because of poor nutrition, non-use or attention deficits. People often fail to think or engage in certain mental activities. The brain may need a "kick" in order to start a mental activity through some kind of stimulus, incentive or source of arousal. It may be the context that determines whether or not urgent thinking is encouraged or provoked. Even feelings that need attention can stimulate selective attention and mental reasoning.

Neuronal (brain cell) networks set up a pathway for specific attention and learning. A pattern of neuronal connections may move ("fire") in some sequence to excite or inhibit signals traveling through the brain. This electrical wiring as it is called, builds up strength on repeated firing and frequent rehearsal. This leads to what is described as brain plasticity - a change in the capacity of the brain to enhance its own mental activity. Receptors or axons are specific molecules in the brain (cells) that recognizes and responds to internal signals. They create an elaborate neural circuitry to transmit information along established brain routes. Learning changes the brain structure and generates new neurons and neuronic connections. The neurons are transmitters that create an electrical force sent to branches of other neurons and circuits. Incoming cognitive units flow easier when there are neuronic patterns or connections that recognize the units in the memory (short or long). There should be other neurons in the system that can respond (be activated) to incoming stimuli (information - images). Otherwise a state of mental ambiguity or sense of temporary dislocation can result when no other information or collateral stimulus is supplied. This is why learning more can create a cross reference mental activity that can draw on different parts of the brain. The less the person knows about a subject the less the stimulating value the subject has. It also means that more activation energy is needed to encourage and facilitate processing of the information at hand. Sometimes low activation or negative activation ("turn off") becomes an inhibitor to further mental (cognitive) response. The mental threshold is too low to lead to the firing (stimulation) of neuronic circuitry and more information processing. This is even more the case when the domain of attention is of little interest or is not familiar. Under these conditions of "attention deficit" the subject domain in question does not get an opportunity to develop an "attention loop" which is a circuit boundary or motivational path that encloses a realm of thinking. This increases in depth and understanding over time as it is used over and over again. Jane Healy reports that motivation is a part of the circuitry system of the brain. Motivation moves to attend (focus) or explore as stimulated ideas engage the mind. Motivation is a key part of metal screening, decision-making, and engagement.

There are mental "template" images and representations used to engage the person's memory in motivational life.

The Thinking Domain

The concept of domain is very important in cognitive theory. A domain is an ordered set of key elements, activities, or factors that define its specialty or function. Each subject, concept or schemata can become a type, category or set called a domain. People learn to think inside of a domain. After much "play" or mental participation the individual develops some domain facility and expertise (such as the mathematical domain). Each domain has its own logic, rules or ways of operating. Domains even have their own terminologies, language and nuances. When individuals master the elements and patterns inside of a field or domain, their intelligence level in that domain increases with time, focus and mental activity. The task is to engage the elements in a particular domain enough so that they become normal to the thinking of that person. Even the mental and social habit – pattern of seeking or pursuing information or a state of being reinforces a mental motivation circuit in place. Often the problem is not intelligence per se, but the will to attend, master and close the intelligence gap inside of any domain. "Gaps" are closed by active, committed persons in pursuit of mastery. Gap closing is a journey or a part of a motivated life that is able to resist distractions.

Templates or coded images, patterns and prototypes are not perfect memory representatives in the mind. They are merely coded mental structures or images that help the mind to make sense of incoming stimuli. They help to speed mental activation and process attention for future recognition and response. A mental activation map is supposed to guide the process towards the template units and excitationary connections. Motivation helps to put the map together for ongoing use. The decision of whether or not to attend to certain subject domains partly resides in what is called unconscious logic created through personal experience. This kind of logic-motivation tendency becomes a pattern or thinking style. People tend to, (especially minority adolescents) move towards and participate in what I call *"domains of convenience"* where they can operate without great effort. These domains of convenience may happen to coincide with apparent natural abilities and personal interest. Convenience domains are influenced by culture and the socialization process. Sometimes the intellectual domain must be superimposed upon the learning process of the adolescent. This is especially true if the domain has not been activated early in the learning process. The person willingly attends to his/her own rules and ways of apprehending and pursuing a particular subject. There are many aspects or elements in various domains that require learning. For example, early grade students need to be encouraged to learn and like mathematics rather than be labeled as incompetent in this domain (or any other domain). This encouragement helps to reduce the amount of felt "distance" the student may feel with the subject at hand. Remember socialization, culture and schooling all affect motivational tendencies.

Psychological distance is enlarged by subconscious or unconscious attitudes and in effective strategies, not incompetence as such. Marilyn Charles asserts that learning from experience is really about setting up a pattern of logic that determines how and what we are going to learn. There is a natural or unnatural logic in each domain that may have to be deconstructed before we are able to apprehend new learning experiences. Patterns of mental logic help determine whether or not we will have intellectual access to certain domains of knowledge or whether we will be able to respond with certain types of our individual mental "templates". How we formulate our thinking patterns affects how we respond to outside stimuli and handle a particular domain.

Past experience helps to organize future responses and the courage necessary to cross the threshold into more challenging avenues or domains of thought. The unfamiliar is not necessarily the most difficult to learn. Any subject that is barely known can be seen as alien to one's comprehension. It is domain familiarity and later mastery that counts. Every would be knower starts out having some kind of knowledge base which helps the knower to know (epistemology). He or she puts this beginning knowledge to work. It is not about feeling comfortable or competent in certain areas but to risk finding one's way around the structured domain of interest. Understanding areas of interest deepens with thought whether they are academic, occupational, spiritual or social. Each domain is a world unto itself. When the elements of a set act or function together they project themselves as an identifiable order or domain. The task is about developing mental habits that would enhance comprehension in each domain. Residual and contextual stimuli can appear to be cognitively inaccessible. But past fears, tragedies, failures and psychic events can surface that affect how people think and learn. A student in the study was called stupid by a teacher in elementary school and he carried that psychological weight for a long time. It turned out he just needed eye glasses. In the meantime, he felt a psychological distance with his subjects. It took several years before his mind could get past that experience and his grades began to improve.

Improved performance is not about making the subject easier. It is about supporting the restructuring of mental patterns of students to make learning (comprehension) easier. Learning occurs through the learner who must process the information given the right effort, attention and encouragement. Thinking is an acquired process. Processing activity helps to construct learning pathways in the mind. It is about building a circuitry and clusters of information for mental reasoning. The encoding system of the brain improves the holding of information and creation of a mental file before decay or extinction of incoming messages occurs.

Sometimes added information aids the cross-over process into other areas that need it. This means that as the student learns more, information can be used in other areas as well. This is cross over. It also refers to the process of brain integration and inter-neuronic (brain cell) activity. The synapses (connections) of the brain can now fire (transmit) in several areas. Brain activity can use one or more sources because of the neurotic connections in memory (Siegel). This transmission process involves both electrical and chemical features. As the knowledge base increases so does the brain's capacity to increase in understanding. The flexibility to address more subject domains puts the learner at a greater advantage.

Different parts of the brain such as the frontal cortex area, primary somesthetic cortex, somesthetic association cortex, are responsible for key "thinking" brain functions (Lynch and Granger). Some areas operate as a specialty area; others operate in conjunction with other brain areas. These areas include the auditory, visual and emotional cortex regions. Other brain areas help to supplement specialty functions when there is a brain injury for example. Parts of the brain help compensate for loses occurring in other areas. One emphasis in this study is to help provide a rationale and strategy for the urgency to improve thinking performance even in the average student who can significantly improve his/her brain power. Those students who have higher hidden potential can do even better. According to Kirby and Paster thinking creates a higher order of understanding but still requires effort. People could think long before they could write. Life begins with thinking not assessment. Assessment is applied to thinking after the fact. Attention leads to thinking. Students need help in turning scattered minds into learning structures. This can also help to improve: abstract (fluid intelligence) reasoning, problem solving, mental speed, (Nisbett) as well as general (g) learning ability (crystallized intelligence). The terms and labels of these operations are not that important, it is the use of brain activity that is the main point.

Attention and Working Memory

Information processing includes the factors of arousal, attention, perception, encoding short-long term memory storage. The concept of working memory came out of short term memory research. The notion of working memory plays a great role in considering adolescent cognition (thinking).

Working memory is defined as a cognition system that functions to deal with specific task on a short term basis. It is concerned with organizing information quickly. Organization takes the form of categories, patterns and stages of problem-solving. Working memory is also considered as a mediator between perceived stimuli and long term memory. Working memory as a type of short term memory has a different circuitry and quality. It is linked to the prefrontal cortex of the brain. It deals chiefly with momentary perceptions and manipulations of incoming current information. This is information that has been selected for attention processing. It gets immediate priority. Priority has to do with forming a quick knowledge structure, facilitating, immediate use of available knowledge. Priority task could be reading, writing, filtering, and assessing, reasoning, rehearsal, planning and problem-solving. It is what we already do on a daily basis.

Working memory includes controlled mental activity which on a neuronic (brain cell) level forms a cluster of neurons which functions as a network of cooperating circuits. This is also called mindfulness (Siegel). Mindfulness involves the brain cooperating with itself. This network of cooperating circuits involves a unique pattern of firing or initiating the transmission of signals through the brain. Mindfulness is an active form of mindset. It includes embedded: values, beliefs, thinking patterns, attitudes, schemas, stress, self-concept, culture, logic, and motives. Mindfulness uses the resources within the mindset to actively explore reality and domains of attention. Mindfulness is reflective and not static and unimaginative. It organizes and reorganizes perceived reality. This is a part of the motivated life and increased well-being. One aspect of adolescence should include more mindfulness and thoughtful explorations. While cognitive activity is occurring there must be a system to make information from other sources in memory available for processing. This is called an episodic buffer which processes stored eventful information from experience and psychological mindfulness.

Working memory cannot be over loaded because it can diminish the mental processing capacity to process more important information. Mental clusters and chunks of information (cramming) cannot form strong group types for easy recall. Working memory must be able to flow unhampered. Stress and stressful conditions hamper mental processing.

The implications of short term memory for the adolescent is that:

Short term memory is very sensitive to distractions, interruptions, and lack of rest. The student must know how to concentrate at the right time to get the best results for later use. Working memory must work.

Short term memory must also be well encoded to help (store) the information until a task is completed. The information may need to be rehearsed in order to lead to effortless processing in similar domains of interest. The information must be recognized before it can be recalled. The information becomes domain friendly for future processing when necessary.

Short term memory especially must have an effective executive manager to navigate timely attention, reflection and reasoning. In short, manipulation of the incoming information must occur early in the process. Decisions and choices may depend upon the ability to manage attention.

The student must engage in mindfulness activity which is a type of ongoing attention and sustained focus in a given domain. This is where effort becomes critical for cultivating a successful thinking and reasoning process. The attention state or mindfulness is an acquired art that must be mastered before higher levels of understanding and processing can occur. Mindfulness helps the brain to create unique neuronic pathways in the learners cognitive system. This also a form of plasticity which leads to new patterns of stimulation response, reflexivity and less decay of unprocessed information.

The student should be able to organize and categorize information for easier comprehension and memorization. Information that is given should not be crammed but systemic and planned in steps. Speed follows the development of mental habits and repeated pathways. Cramming jams too many things together and short circuits the process. Students and teachers should avoid information overloads by using logical conceptual planned sequences. People learn better in steps.

Effort, Thinking, and Culture

The benefits of increasing attention in a given area of interest (domains) are: sharpened perception, better retention, and an increase in the speed of thought. There is also a decrease of the effects of learning problems (Doidge). The great number of activities going on in the brain simultaneously requires a decisive effort to regulate, increase, inhibit and/or process information. The mind is the processor of experience and consciousness. It contains both experience as a form of thought and activates engaged stimuli at the same time. The "effort system" incorporates a larger set of governing attention factors (Jarvis). Processing current information must compete against subconscious episodes as past experiences within memory. Negative or traumatic experiences can become a part of the self-hood of the person. These experiences can act as interfering data that is included in mental deliberations. The thinking mind includes ongoing contact with the world past and present. The mind must be free to think clearly and selectively about current matters of interest. This takes effort.

Doidge also says that another factor in improving attention and thinking is the bicultural factor. This line of investigation has highlighted the mental effect of two or more competing social cultures. Learning includes the process of acculturation. This means that the culture that embeds the mind-set of the person informs how the person receives and processes information. W.E.B. Dubois refers to the double consciousness of the negro. A type of thinking-learning style develops in the maturing, cultural individual. The individual is in fact a person of history and culture. Whenever a different culture is encountered new domains and ways of thinking reflect this culture. There are differences in held values and ideas receiving critical attention. Crossing over from one culture and intellectual domain to another is not to be taken lightly. It is a challenge in itself. The brain uses the culture it has acquired. Culture is wired into our thinking. Culture modifies brain circuitry. In a suitable manner culture shapes lines of reasoning and memories that become natural to the person's cognitive make up. When a person is assimilated into a culture so is his or her ways of thinking. This is one reason that testing and measuring the intelligence of people is a sensitive matter. The strength of individual effort must exceed the person's inner resistance to accommodate new global thinking and domains. It is like a paradigm shift for many. Effort control and attention regulation is needed to reinforce mindfulness and connection with specific domains of study. This may involve a cross-over crisis. Learners often experience domain crisis when intimidated.

The Seduction of Focus

Margaret Wetherell a social psychologist argues that social-culture influences are pervasive and inescapable. The social-cultural environment stimulates the level and quality of individual awareness, beliefs and psychological well-being. The environment contains seductive influences coming from language (a way of seeing reality) ideology, meanings and technology that are used in the context. Culture is seen as a complex of borrowed traits (Kuper). This is why Eric Jensen asserts that the attempt to separate nurture and nature (genetics) is ineffective because the environment, nutrition and life style can have a major impact upon mental plasticity. Violence, isolation, drugs, abuse, depression, prejudice and trauma can have negative effects upon mental performance. Once the person begins to acquire or process significant amounts of intimidating stimuli he/she tends to become more unstable, in cohesive, and dysfunctional.

These influences help organize one's way of life. The self is embedded in the social-cultural matrix. Images or signals in the social context feed into the way the brain receives and organizes information. This can affect the pursuit of the motivated life. The brain uses culture to encode and prepare representation for human memory. Culture is an elusive factor along with other factors. Culture is a strong seductive factor in human development. Cultural ideas may oppose the growth and transformation process of the individual.

This is why the study demonstrated that for many adolescents each step in the goal-setting process took significant will and effort. Each step involved an act of fortitude and courage because of different cultural and mental styles of processing information. Each step, from awareness to goal implementation took a certain kind of assessment and action. The time line for step by step transition was not certain or unproblematic for these adolescents. This is why student counsel and feedback is important. Each step of awareness and decision-making is dependent upon "attending". Attention giving is also a means of developing inquiry skills, or depth of observations, analysis and participation in a given domain. The student becomes mindful of the details and relevance of careful study as the brain develops mental pathways to increased learning and reduces anxiety.

In summation, there is a difference between academic success and cultural success. Some students in the school system were experiencing academic failure or disappointment. At the same time many of them felt quite at home engaging in cultural life. Culture has its own definition of success and acceptance. The individual feels connected to his/her culture and committed to engage in self-affirming cultural life. This often includes a common world view language, games and creative leisure inherent in the culture.

This participation becomes effortless participation. But the domain of academic success requires great effort, a different kind of thinking and neuronic routes (brain circuitry). The information that is needed to participate in academic life is different from the information available in cultural life. Each domain that utilized helps to shape different patterns of thinking. Student life consist of developing a knowledge structure that supports academic thinking.

New Predispositions about academic participation must also be accompanied by changes in institutional life as well. There should be a validating context in school life for students whose confidence and record of academic success is weak. In other words student progress should be documented and affirmed by the teaching staff as feed back. The adolescent exists in a complex changing society. He or she may or may not get the needed help in time to make a real difference in his or her educational journey. New cognitive reflexive patterns (habits) and higher levels of thinking should lead to higher levels of interest and performance.

Learning Attribution and Testing

Attribution is the linking of event with cause and outcome. Attribution occurs through reflection of both a state or activity with perceived results. This type of linked conclusion is important for motivational choices and strategies. Behavior is explained in light of something referred to before or after an action is taken or declined. The person mentally and emotionally refers to certain factors that inform why he or she believes that effort does or does not pay off for a given task.

The individual may believe for example, that the task is too difficult, is not relevant, takes too long or requires too much preparation at the time. The task may require a high level of ability (competence) or is not worth the social risk of embarrassment in case of failure. Therefore, the face value of the task is informed by past memories and a cognitive attitude towards certain kinds of challenges and domains. It takes courage, confidence and mental readiness to tackle certain academic subjects and fields. Sometimes others will lead students to lower their ambitions (goals). This is the easy way out.

Student attribution can result from the results of IQ tests. Jenson reports that original IQ tests were designed to measure potential school success and not for reality (real-world) testing. The 0.05 correlation results of some key testing indicate that 75% of the grade variance for example, is attributable to factors beyond intelligence (Jensen). Intelligence test tended to measure analytic, creative and practical ability. The analytic category requires more selective attention and is emphasized the most. Few students understand what the test really means in regards to their own abilities. The "g" Factor in cognitive theory does mean that persons of general or average intelligence can enhance their own brain performance. Even genes have been found to have more flexibility in affecting other genes, hormones, cognition, learning and behavior. This expressive function of genes called the transcription factor is environmentally sensitive so that environment has a significant role to play. What this all means again, is that each factor affects other factors. The combination of interacting factors cannot precisely predict the potential of the entire domain of human intelligence. Test results are based upon test content, wording, logic, format, and cultural assumptions. To speak of intelligence gaps assumes an intellectual position about many intervening factors.

Learning is a responsive process. The learner, teacher, and learning situation is a living dynamic that has a life of its own. It is a dynamic interchange. Arousal can be lost in a monotonous, unresponsive environment. Feedback steps helps the student to encode positive template types of information with understanding. Positive attribution is heavily centered on teacher expectation, changing mental attitudes, increased cognitive engagement, reduction of cognitive distance, and mental rehearsal with paired (multiple) stimuli. Streams of coordinated activities that support student interest, approval, effort, and attention help provide a frame-work for greater, cognitive exploration.

The study has emphasized the ongoing need to think even if no goals were in mind. Bandura has argued that thinking helps to prepare the person to develop cognitive competencies, self-efficacy and future aspirations. Thinking involves entertaining possible rewards for effort and self-initiatives. As the person thinks a sense personal responsibility and self-ownership can occur over time. Thinking is the beginning of taking charge over one's life. The study has shown that as the students began to think about their plight, they also began to act. They began to move towards goal-setting.

Wider perspectives and intentional behavior emerge out of personal reflection and critical thinking. The thinking person who examines life on an increasingly wider perspective develops the mental capacity or tools to make better assessments and more accurate attributions. That is they can link cause and outcome with better clarity. Sub-goals can be effectively put in place to reach larger goals. Gradual steps can be put in place as a part of a total process. This process is more clearly seen after reflection. There is less ambiguity and apprehension when manageable units are pursued. In terms of brain plasticity, learning and doing by steps enables mental growth to occur because brain synapses (connections) and neurotransmitters can better reinforce and process information through neuro circuits. Action potentials or nerve impulses create travel routes that increase recognition, learning and mental recall of information. Memory codes develop distinctive ways of encoding and transmitting information. Ongoing brain input helps determine how the brain is organized. The brain through continuous input becomes physiologically dedicated to a particular domain. Learning is amplified through focused attention (Schwartz and Begley).

In short, attending, thinking and engaging in information-processing still takes effort. Rather than worry about testing gaps, the task is not to catch up with generalized others but to catch up with one's self. Each student has his or her own mental potential beyond test scores. If a student does not access that potential and exploit his or her own brain capacity, how others perform can be irrelevant. Intelligence is "activity dependent" no matter how much potential a person may have. The concern is to shorten the cognitive distance between student thinking and environmental cues/resources. A developmental program needs to be devised to accomplish this task. The motivated student is one who first of all makes an effort. The student wills to confront his or her own well-being and success through meaningful action. The other elements of motivation such as: ability, skills, beliefs, incentives, rewards, persistence, arousal, teacher feedback and self-esteem all converge once interest and effort is generated. Effort pulls all of the relevant factors together in a network of motivation that helps to structure and stabilize the pursuit of goals and "achievement" (success).

Motivation, Effort and Attention Summary

This study centers on motivation. However, motivation can increase mental ability and learning. Daniel Amen, MD reports that when forethought occurs in the prefrontal cortex (executive brain) it excites motivation. Increased passion and excitement from a stimulus increases dopamine. Dopamine is a chemical that is activated by passion and emotion. It is associated with motivated attention, decisions, positive rewards, and reinforcements. (Amen, Willis). Motivation increases personal propensity to achieve and set goals through a willingness and effort to think. The person must continue the process of excitement and brain stimulation. Opportunities to achieve increase as the capacity of the individual to focus more and understand more increases. Encouragement does not replace a thought out reason to perform. It doesn't take the place of thinking and engaging the area of concentration. The intelligence to perform a task involves selective attention and reasonable thinking as the linking of ideas. A "train of thought" must begin that connects an array of perceptions and meaningful associations (Wartik, Carlso-Finnerty). Ongoing attention and thought leads to developing a style (pattern) of thinking that increases with brain plasticity.

Motivated concerns, interest and effort increase the speed of encoding in working memory where attention is seriously applied. Obscure or unstimulating domains can become "domain friendly" and "psychological distance" is shortened. Mastery of specific domains are related to motivational states and dispositions toward learning. Dispositions are acquired traits and patterns. These dispositions can in time create unique styles of learning and processing of information through strengthening of mental circuitry as we have discussed. Students should not avoid subjects that seem to be difficult without giving them serious attention. This is the challenge!

Motivation seeks and searches (Simon). Attention notices and processes selective (filtered) information. The strength of motivation and effort contribute to the ability of the student to overcome distractions and mental competition with other thoughts and people. The presence of goals also helps to sustain attention. External or extrinsic incentives help to encourage motivational interest. Extrinsic stimulation can become intrinsic motivation during periods of active thinking. Extrinsic and intrinsic motivation, we have argued, tend to make artificial distinctions in the cognitive process. Performances which seem to show a lack of motivation or disinterest be encouraged from external sources in the environment. Negative sources tend to drive down (de-motivate) possible interest in significant domains. Positive external incentives can arouse intrinsic tendencies that may be present already. Intrinsic motivation is best accomplished in a free-flowing, less problematic environment. Overly charged contexts, marginal living, a lack of relevant knowledge base war against the liberty of deeper reflection and intrinsic innovation. This is why subcultures must create their own expressions of human meaning. Human attention and psychic energy is invested in different domains of expression fluidity. This is the source of intrinsic motivation.

Environmental impact is especially important to contextually sensitive persons (which adolescents tend to be). Many factors work together to create a composite influence that can encourage, discourage or limit motivation, performance and ultimately mental capacity. This study has in fact discussed many factors involved in goal-setting orientation and the motivated life.

Motivation, effort and attention are not just beneficial for goal-setting and success, but to the entire realm of cognitive and social growth. Motivation encourages the individual to engage in a life-time activity, not just to attend school. This activity includes inquiry, exploration, appraisal and discovery on all levels. Cognitive development is strengthened through the habit of organizing incoming information which can lead into abstract thinking and conjuncture. In this life-world you must think. This is a world of deception and distortions. Cognitive activity moves into the unknown from information that is known. This movement consists of pushing ideas and concepts around in the mind. It is a form of reasoning, perception and learning (Novack & Gowin). As reflection occurs unique features and attributes of the subject are more clearly seen through the redundancy of attention and thinking. The construction of new knowledge helps in finding one's way around information and global concepts that are needed. Learning becomes evident as adaptation occurs. Adaptation is the process of gathering, organizing and using information from the environment in order to succeed. This again is a part of the motivated life style. This information is put to use as directed actions (Hettema). The individual is able to take various levels of information and complex ideas and apply them to goal-tasks. Information becomes a resource for motivated ends. Desired information affects the disposition of the person to learn because it has reward-incentive power. The information of interest must be viewed as relevant to personal well-being and goals. It is incorporated into the person's memory-knowledge base. In time this knowledge base helps to shape the individual's personality.

In all areas of life the individual needs to pay attention to information and activities will affect his or her life. Motivation is contextually embedded. There are "push and pull" factors in the environment that also impact on attention. People tend to adopt task-goals modeled in the environment. Any desired state or goal requires autonomy, (effort) and social intelligence. That is individuals must know how the environment works. Each person must create a "dispositional structure" within his or her own personality (cognitive process). This structure reinforces the acting out of rehearsed mental goals which becomes useful can confront social reality. Disposition, values intention and effort must be integrated in personality as a process. The person will have a motivated mind and tendency to act. The motivated life really includes a modified cognitive structure and personality that is predisposed to think and manage. A disposition as a willingness to perform consistently must be encouraged and developed in the adolescent. Each person who would succeed in a world with a parade of obstacles and mazes (confusing networks and hidden complexities) must develop an intentional pattern of applied meaning to personal tasks and goals. When true motivational patterns begin to unfold and the executive function of the mind begins to pursue certain goals. The Motivated Life has started.

Cognitive Learning Chart

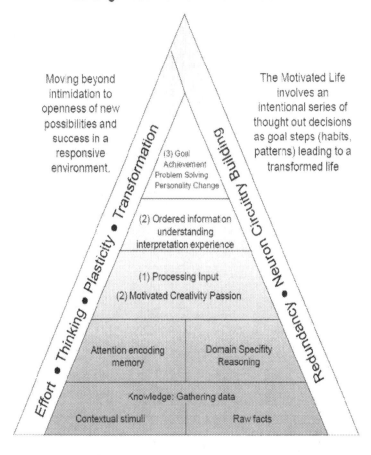

Cognitive Learning Chart

Reducing Psychological Distance

Willing Attentive Engagement

Thinking Motivation and Achievement

Moving beyond intimidation to openness of new possibilities and success in a responsive environment.

The Motivated Life involves an intentional series of thought out decisions as goal steps (habits, patterns) leading to a transformed life

Transformation

Building Neuron Circuitry Building

Plasticity

Thinking

Redundancy

Effort

(3) Goal Achievement Problem Solving Personality Change

(2) Ordered information understanding interpretation experience

(1) Processing Input

(2) Motivated Creativity Passion

Attention encoding memory

Domain Specifity Reasoning

Knowledge: Gathering data

Contextual stimuli

Raw facts

Intelligence Enhancement Processing Building Mental Structures Confidence and Competence

CHAPTER 7
CONCLUSION: STUDY RESULTS
AND FUTURE PLANNING

Introduction: Goal-Setting, Coping
Adolescents and the Motivated Life

The central idea of this study is the need to achieve a more meaningful existence in the context in which we live. Adolescents and adults should strive to engage in crafting a motivated life style that can lead to higher level of personal well-being and achievement. Motivational life is a rhythm of action. It is seeing life as a connected whole.

> The motivational life involves intentions, routines, good habits, and a creative mindset (mindfulness). It is about how your everyday life is organized and carried out. It is about how you use your energy, time, and talents. This involves how you solve your problems, handle your stress, and get excited.

This study on goal setting was initiated because motivational life is extremely important in a complex society; Adolescents and adults in urban society have particular social, personal and academic problems. The study was undertaken to deal with contemporary factors in society that affect motivational tendencies of urban male students. The challenge is now to move beyond crisis obsession to a meaningful, productive life.

The purpose of the inquiry was to gain more understanding about motivation principles in general and urban high school students in particular. The study included a local high school, a local neighborhood, related statistics, and the individual perspectives of students in the study. The results of this research have spin-offs for others as well. This investigation endeavored to understand more about the contemporary world in which adolescents live and cope. It was not meant to generalize to everyone. Coping is an element of well-being and survival. It involves ongoing responsive cognitive and behavioral efforts in the dynamic urban context (Brides). Adolescents must deal with constantly changing contextual demands that seem to exceed their personal resources. This frustration was expressed in the study. Implications of the study relate to difficulties in the educational, and economic domains which are faced by many reasons. Other related factors are at work, such as inequity, universal well-being, and global politics. All of these factors can be analyzed by utilizing the insights of current research and applied critical theory. These factors will be discussed. Concepts related to the study like "scientific indicators of well-being" provided an opportunity to examine society on a more comprehensive level. These indicators are social markers; they point out factors that help explain the nature of personal experiences in the environment by looking at the bigger picture.

Information was sought in order to gain a more in-depth picture of the contextual life that might impact upon goal-setting tendencies of male urban adolescents. The study helped to gain information about the way these adolescents encounter the world and respond to challenges. After conducting the study, several significant patterns and educational conditions were observed that helped to explain the ongoing social plight of these urban male adolescents and young adults.

Discussion of the Findings: Thinking Through the Data

The findings of the study fall into three categories: Goal-setting and success; adolescent school life and performance (the educational journey of the adolescent); and contextual reality in the urban social environment.

This discussion of the findings of the study will start with goal-setting and success and continue on to school life and performance, and finally to the contextual reality of the students. After the findings of the study are discussed, there will be a discussion about the larger social picture, the role of the school, critical theory, and a goal-incentive program. The discussion will include emphasis for future research, goal-setting theory, and the literature.

Looking Forward: Goal-Setting and Success

Since the notion of success is an important concept in the adolescent community, the study began with a success survey. A short survey and discussion was conducted among 20 high school students by an assistant researcher. The survey was entitled: "What is success to you?" In response, no student connected success to education or a career track. The responses generally centered around personal feelings, social status, well-being, and self-respect. Even in the test interviews, the question about success usually centered around feeling free, having prosperity, and being something. Tyson said: "I want to make an impact in society so people can see there is something to me." This is a social goal.

Tyson and others in the study focused on success and not achievement. Success was about life and overcoming social stigmas. This was form of looking forward in that it involved dealing with the resolution of present concerns. In the study the adolescent did not usually set any goals without first considering his subjective and contextual situation. Black adolescents were aware of mainstream social attitudes and condescending views about them. This knowledge came directly from social encounters, media, and family communications. This did not mean that the adolescents were not interested in achievement; they were not interested in achievement in isolation from real life and well-being. The need for success and good school performance developed in steps. Utility values related to "achievement" in time became a useful means of problem solving and goal setting for the adolescents involved in the study.

Time Thinking and Goal-Setting Tendencies:
Think Before You Sink

The study did show that the immediate state of the respondents informed their future anticipated needs. The future was a reconstruction of current needs projected into the future. In the same manner, the respondents of the study reflected upon their past. They used their interpreted views of their experiences and hardships to help decide future need-states and goals. This is one reason why well-being and success were major concerns in the study. Social goals, personal values, well-being, and futuristic expectations were all a part of the gaps found in the literature.

Present mental and emotional images or schemes of past experiences helped the students to decide on the possible merits of any goal setting. Past events such as struggles for survival, avoidance of arrest or street trouble, and economic hardship often served as triggers or goal activators in constructing the ideals of subjective well-being and success. In other words, a cognitive (mental) scheme and way of thinking informed adolescents' aspirations. Jones argues in the literature that Blacks are affected by their social experiences in planning their lives and anticipating future rewards. Social experience and episodic events do affect adolescent anticipations. The move towards setting goals occurred in steps for those in the study.

Time for many adolescents in the study revolved around the interpreted "historic moment." The decision to look backward, to engage in present interpretations of life, to remain indecisive about the future, or to move forward, became a challenge. In this light, the need for school achievement for future success gradually became important for some students in the study.

The concept of academic achievement was not the key motive for adolescent success in the study. Nor was the idea of climbing the social and corporate ladder of major concern to these students. As much time that they spent much in school every year of high school, they still did not connect their futures with schooling. The merging of academic performance goal setting and success was not necessarily an immediate consideration in the minds of these students. One student remarked that it took effort just to go to school. This was a form of success.

Goal-Setting and School: Line Up

A major finding was the state of intellectual and academic apathy among the students in the study. Many students felt almost disoriented and indifferent to school and future planning. This condition was accompanied by a lack of direction, goal-setting, and futuristic expectations by the students. The students acknowledged their state of non-readiness and unpreparedness upon entry to high school. Many of these adolescents said in effect that the middle school experience was a waste. It was uneventful and nonproductive for many adolescents. The few students who were prepared came from more educated homes. The study found that whatever the background of the parents was (they were usually of the working class), most parents endorsed strong academic performance. But this did not usually happen, at least in a timely way. Some students had advanced to the upper grades in high school before they began to take school seriously. The students interviewed appeared to go through stages of interest and awareness before they began to reflect, decide, and follow up on setting goals for their future. Students differed in their pace for pursuing higher levels of educational performance.

This orientation or pattern is called ambiguity in the study. The state of ambiguity included feelings of vagueness and dislocation regarding academic preparation and direction. The school and early life experience did not generate any great sequential movement towards personal development or school achievement. The middle school in particular was a journey of ambiguity. This journey clearly foreshadowed motivational inertia, as discussed already. There was a lack of specific attention in various subjects.

It was not surprising that it took a great deal of effort to reverse the trend of apathy, school failure, and mediocrity. This change involved a cognitive makeover. The adolescent started his high school career under a handicap of unreadiness and inadequate preparation. This led to a more or less permanent assignment to a lower educational track. It also led into a catch-up perspective rather than a futuristic perspective. The students and counselors felt the student should strive to "get out of high school" to avoid a complete loss. It was not about realizing ones' fullest potential, but about expediency.

The next observation that emerged out of the study was that goal setting was a gradual process of steps, each of which required a major effort for many students in the school study. The goal process showed that some adolescents would often name a goal, but did not exert any meaningful effort to attain the goal. Often some kind of "push" was needed to complete the process. There was very little push or personal involvement by teachers and staff. The study did show that some adolescents tended to respond to extrinsic rewards of encouragement as a push or challenge to move on and achieve. Intrinsic motivation tended to follow extrinsic stimulation and incentives. The adolescents were aware of their negative social stigmas. These stigmas often contributed to their uncertain academic self-esteem. The students felt a strong need to maintain and pursue a strong sense of well-being and success as they responded to external conditions.

Goal-Setting in the Urban Context

The study also showed a combination of hindering factors in the social environment, such as: boring school programs, the lack of family resources, and bad personal habits (TV, hanging out, lack of sleep, inadequate homework time). These factors together constituted a downward trajectory. A negative trajectory which is a loosely connected series of personal and environmental occurrences that leads to lower academic interest and performance. In light of social and personal challenges that were prevalent, the adolescent did not always develop good coping strategies. They often disengaged themselves from the learning process. In the study, once students reflected on their failing performance some of them began to take corrective measures. They made a decision. They also made an effort to set goals and engage in a process of self-regulation. It became a challenge to reverse the student's habits because their academic mind-set or cognitive structure which had been dormant over a period of time. Therefore, a decision to enact a change of focus and direction also included a change in ways of thinking. The goal-setting process was then carried out. Behavioral adjustment changes or new corrective patterns are difficult to carry out.

Future Research

There are many areas for future research. These areas include a study of the direct or indirect impact of environmental forces on the life of the adolescent. More study needs to be conducted on the role of the middle school (passage dynamics) and the unprepared adolescent. Studies of intervention strategies are needed to explore ways to break the cycle of apathy, ambiguity, and dead-end trajectories in the life of the adolescent. Research needs to be done on how and what resources can be applied by educators to help the adolescent establish and maintain self-defining goal-setting activity.

School related questions that need to be answered include: What are the best ways to minimize transitional trauma from middle school to high school. There is a need for more preparation. So many students drop out in the 9th grade. There are students who may not want to be locked into an assigned track. Some students become interested in their future or education on a delayed, gradual basis. Flexibility is needed for these students who may be late bloomers.

An important challenge for the public school is to determine what it can do to create interest, motivation, and goal striving in urban adolescents who do not have adequate knowledge or preparation. Monk stated that: "We are not programmed to deal with society". Students want relevant education and direction. Even when students decide to make an effort to get out of high school it is in part a response to contextual (extrinsic) factors. This includes survival and the avoidance of the embarrassment of failure, more than it is about education in school. Pragmatic considerations and contextual incentives move the student to complete requirements for a basic diploma. It was not the school itself that operated as the prime motivator of goal setting and academic achievement. School performance was not necessarily seen as a major factor in attaining a successful life. Contextual ideas often became a catalyst for goal-setting activities for students in the study.

Goal setting is not a one-dimensional problem. It is about finding one's way around in a competitive world and making one's own decisions under "fair" conditions. This focus helps to lead the adolescent into facing the future through goal-setting behavior. Added burdens of negotiating negative environments and accompanying negative feelings are difficult to manage. The student must adjust to his environment as "the other" in society and gain respect in the process. Further research about goal setting should include "relevant" education, the responsive environment, and the mental and emotional state of the adolescent. The adolescent must learn how to engage different domains of study with an open mind.

Critical Theory: Indications of Social Struggle and Well-Being

Critical theory deals with looking at the lives of people against the background of actual conditions in the social order. It provides a way of looking at social forces behind human suffering, pain, disadvantages, and conflict with social structures (Lemert). Critical theory examines sources of social contradiction and power relationships. It also deals with patterns that lead to restricted life and limited attainment. Critical observation requires that persons view each other against the reality of world conditions and threats to their quality of life. Well-being is affected by mindset, emotional state, self-regulation, stress levels, a sense of intrinsic cohesion and motivational orientation. These factors help to determine what the quality of life will be like.

Critical theory asks: Under what assumptions are the actors performing or not performing in the social order. For example: what were you thinking when you made that decision? Relevant questions are raised so that liberating strategies can result from unfolding self-defining ideas that informed adolescent notions about well-being. It does not follow that the success of a few individuals indicates the success of the many who are socially overwhelmed and cannot "see" where they are going.

There are questions about underperformance in urban life. Adolescents, public schools, and urban social structures all tend to underperform (Anyon). There are social contradictions and rules of operating that lie behind the economic and educational plight of struggling urban dwellers and their families (J. Wilson). Society makes occupational and academic demands upon its constituents, yet it under prepares them. The study shows background factors relating to African American family struggles, (economic, legal, political, etc.). These factors indicate that a complex of underperforming institutions affect individual performance. The macro affects the micro life patterns of its constituencies. The arrest record, for example, is higher for adolescents than it is for any other age group. There are few jobs and planned recreation facilities after school. The illegal drug traffic seems to exist unabated after so many years. In the study area special community programs were initiated to help local residents navigate the legal system. There are so many legal matrices on many levels families cannot adjudicate simple legal matters.

As I reported earlier, many students in the study talked about their family challenges. Eston said, "My mom is a nurse's aide and is constantly working. She is not around much". Monk stated that his "biggest obstacle is fear, the fear of death" (by violence). Rhad reported that "this is a bad neighborhood. There are drug dealers, fights, and cops. People are afraid to call the police because of what may happen to them" (if they call). Fason stated that his "mother works downtown in security from 12 p.m. to 8 p.m. I grew up learning how to live without money". Swan said that his "mother works in a nursing home". William said that: "right now, I am not successful. I don't have ten dollars in my pocket

. . . In society you have to fight for fairness. Even if you get educated you (Black people) are still nothing". Peterson reported that: "It is noisy late at night with guns and fights. This is hard when you have to go to school the next day. . .my mother works hard. She works two jobs. She works in nursing". There were many revealing narratives.

Perry, Steele, and Hilliard reported in the literature that there is a strong possibility that high schools can play a detrimental role in fostering disengagement by adolescent students because of the cultural organization of the school, rather than peer pressure that is sometimes cited in some of the literature. The social context embodies an invisible, underemphasized power of institutional culture. This contextual relationship affects how individuals think and perform. Pinnock, who is the son of middle-class professional parents, acted very serious during the interview. Usually the students were very informal. He stated: "I liked my middle school experience a lot. It was pleasant. My teachers were very helpful. They gave me personal attention...We had a good relationship". Apparently, again, the more the student blends in with mainstream mannerisms, appearance, and speech, the more he or she tends to be accepted and helped by the mainstream culture.

The concept of goal-directedness states that while the individual strives to achieve goals, social values and contextual norms influence how that process is going to be carried out. People are somewhat dependent upon conditions in the environment. Society provides invisible guidelines that affect individual pursuits. The predisposition of the person meets the normative impact of society. This encounter affects different people in different ways. Outcomes are strongly influenced by the disposition of the individual.

Carr and MacLachlan maintain that there is a motivational gravity or push and pull that is exerted upon individuals in the social context. There are factors that can encourage or discourage individual motivation. This concept becomes critical when subordinate persons are undervalued. This kind of situation can affect goal-setting tendencies.

Bargh and Gollwitzer reported that people respond to environmental states which trigger or affect goal-directed behavior. It was Monk who said: "Society is a bad place and you don't want others telling you what to do". Chronic situations in particular affect how people anticipate environmental difficulties or opportunities in attaining future results. The environment itself is a form of ongoing communications. People can be prompted to act or evaluate life as a consequence of participating in social or cultural environments. For example, by observing adverse conditions students are turned off to mainstream avenues of success. By participating in hip-hop music and its messages, the student associates popular artists with status, power, and success. This kind of mental association sets the pattern for future social relationships and non-educational ways to become successful. Hip-hop music serves as a means to offset and refute persuasive social hegemonies and contradictions.

One reason why critical theory is so important is that its significance includes, but reaches beyond, the plight of youth in the local environment. For those who ask if Black adolescents have problems because they are Black and don't seek to achieve, the study tends to show that the constellation of factors, not ethnicity alone, that complicates adolescent problems. Adolescents who have strong family and school support tend to have better academic performance. Composite indicators of race, class, gender, context, schools, and personality, with economic and political policies together produce a unique case of the coping urban male. It is not a single-factor problem. It is a multilevel and multi-faceted problem. This is why it is not easy to solve.

Critical theory is also important because the theory recognizes that a "successful society" doesn't mean that most of the people in that society are successful (Dienert & Suh). The well-being and social condition of individuals need to be analyzed and explained. As the nature of the global economic context (labor market) of groups change, the mobility of adolescents moving towards self-support is going to be more challenging.

Dienert and Suh claim that societies in the world are becoming more democratized. Democracy is becoming a more universal way of life. At the same time, people are becoming more sensitive to their subjective well-being. People want the freedom and autonomy to seek the more successful life. Well-being, according to Dienert and Suh, is a particularly democratic feature. People are more inclined to engage in self-reflective evaluation than to look to a power elite for just options and regulation. Society has an obligation to help its constituents to succeed in the global world. The concern for what constitutes the ideal life is becoming the consideration of a wider public. People who cannot reach their goals and live out their values will become less satisfied and more problematic. Davidson, Rosenberg, and Moore argue that leadership and a social will are needed to improve social determinants of well-being. These determinants include existing social disparities, treatment of children, health care, and the dispensing of information technology. They argue that decision makers should know and utilize information that works to help communities become more successful. This success would improve the general well-being of the community.

Hip-Hop and Social Struggle

I spent some time dealing with the issue of whether or not Black youth had by adolescence developed an ideology. The word "ideology" seemed too strong (formal) to apply to this group. The research showed no indications of a formal ideology. I felt convinced that the term should not be used in regards to most urban adolescents because they did not articulate a systematic body of connected ideas or strong feelings about society and its politics. There were comments about unfairness and prejudice, but there was no indication of a formal system of social and political thought in the minds of the adolescents in the study. Success, survival and respect was more of a concern than covering the right global discourse.

In the course of the investigation, a slightly open door about hip-hop as leisure in the interviews led to a better understanding about adolescents, hip-hop, and ideology. In his book on cultural theory and popular culture, John Storey explores several ideas about popular culture that are relevant to the study.

Social images and impressions about reality help to form a body of ideas and practices that are associated with these images. These cultural images attempt to show how the world really is. This body of ideas or ideology is not one of ideas alone. It is lived as ritual, identity, customs, and patterns of behavior (Storey). This body of ideas defines its own world of language, images, thoughts, logic, and practices. In hip-hop culture, this body of thought deals with social contradictions and hegemony. Hegemony consists of one-sided ideas from mainstream society. Hip-hop culture offers alternate ways of seeing the world. Hip-hop creates its own images of the world. Hip-hop expresses styles of speech, myths, dress, and discourse. It becomes in fact a social ideological form. It becomes a structure of voice and power. Hip-hop even generates its own economy and success stories. When some adolescents in the study participated in the world of hip-hop, they were in fact participating in a live form of ideology. They acted out ideology. The question is: Does this ideology affect goal-setting focus and academic performance? This relationship can become a research project.

What Can We Do: Goal-Setting Incentive Program

After reviewing the main aspects of the results of the study the question arises: What can we do about it? This program proposal is a possible way to move from research on to practice. The study indicates that many students are at a great disadvantage in dealing with their futures, and the school system is not able to deal with their "personal issues". There needs to be a program dealing with motivation and goal setting. The study on goal-setting motivation should lead to some type of incentive program. Students need a more personal and relevant approach to their plight. An approach has been formulated from information obtained from the study. The purpose of the program is to promote an adolescent self-starter group. This program consists of activities, interactions, and group stimulation exercises. Since adolescents often function well in groups, this program will encourage group sharing and cooperation. The pilot study on success was an informal group session, it produced valuable insights on related adolescent views. This approach is not necessarily the only approach to motivation awakening. Educators can choose or devise the method that seems to work best for them. This method reflects goal-setting stages that resulted from the research.

In regards to the schooling experience of the adolescents, the students came into the high school in a state of ambiguity, mediocrity, or motivational inertia. Many students either were not satisfied with their school performance or were unsatisfied with it and did little about it. It then became the task of their high school career to play catch-up to attain a higher academic level. Most of the African American students in the school were assigned to the general program. This is a nonspecific program that does not prepare the student for a particular goal, career, trade, profession, school, or occupation. It is a general program for the general, average, unintentional student with a poor to fair record. Once in this program, students usually remained until they graduated or dropped out. Most do not "catch up". They are structured in.

In regards to the environment, the students and public records reported much violence, unemployment, underemployment, health concerns, gangs, and community–police relations concerns. Many students did not like the neighborhood they were living in. Some students felt they were living a life under duress. Therefore a program needs to be put in place that is relevant to their contextual reality. The suggested goal-enhancement program that follows is designed to refocus the student away from oppressive conditions and thinking to engage in a personal process of gradual self-development. This takes effort. This takes mentorship skills.

Incentive Program Outline

The task or the aim of the goal-setting enhancement program is to help move the student through goal steps (observed in the study) to goal completion. The program is based upon the research results that indicate that the students were involved in several phases or steps before any meaningful goal outcomes became evident.

The first challenge was to help push or encourage the student to think about his situation. The adolescent is to be encouraged to engage in reflections, evaluation, and decision making. Not all the students were in a state of total apathy, yet many of them were unable to make an effort to improve their school performance or adopt "realistic" goals. Some did not even have serious aspirations about their future. Bordan, for example, made a statement similar to other statements in the study. He said: "Up until high school (grade 10) there was little to motivate me to do anything but attend. I did just enough to get by. My average was C's and D's." Tyson, grade 10, reported: "I have recently gotten serious about education. I was just getting by." Themos, grade 10, only had a 69 average and stated: "My obstacle is that I doubt myself. I procrastinate. I can't seem to finish anything." Therefore it can be very productive in the right communal setting.

Program Structure

The sessions begin with 15 to 20 students seated in a circle formation. There are also young adult facilitators present to guide discussions. Students are selected from a list of screened volunteers. Qualifications for entry into the program consist of readiness for self-improvement, a past record of low performance (or underperformance), and availability for full participation in the four-week program. Each session will have a specific focus. Topics may, however, run over into another session. The program is designed to have meaningful content, flow, and challenge. The program is also designed not to be overwhelming in terms of assignment so that the purpose of reflection and decision making can be accomplished without producing a stressful climate.

Goal-Setting Incentive Steps and Sessions: Moving Beyond Diffused Minds

Personal Awareness Session. During this session students will discuss their "issues," concerns, and present stance. What did growing up in the city teach me? What do I need to avoid? Where am I now and what shall I focus on? The student is expected to move beyond personal ambiguity to attention and particularity of interest. What is it the student can do to overcome the challenges of the past? This session is a response to the state of ambiguity and adolescent laxity shown in the study.

The World That I Face Session. Students in the study desired education that was relevant to what they had to face in the world. This session will deal pragmatically with the relevant environment the student sees or comes to see during the session. The focus will move from personal awareness to global awareness. The question for this session is: What is going on in the world (society) now that will affect my future?

How is society organized? What do employers want? What recent business and political events have emerged that impact upon my life? Assigned readings will be shared.

What challenges do I face in the environment? What three obstacles do I face in becoming successful? The group will discuss obstacles, hindrances, and strategies for facing goal challenges. This part responds to the need of adolescents to make decisions after serious thinking about their personal predicaments. Feedback reinforces the merit of engaging attention in specific areas.

Students in the study provided subjective definitions for success. But success must also be assessed in global terms. What does success mean in facing environmental challenges? Questions to be considered include: Can I devise a strategy to become successful in a larger context? What would that strategy look like? What happens if my strategy fails to get me where can I go? How can I relate the desire for success to personal ability attention and achievement? What lessons can hip-hop artists teach us about risk and success? What is good or bad about their success? The next session relates to the "effort state" and the pursuit of goal pathways. The adolescent seeks a way to concretize or apply the idea of success for his life.

Building a Sub-Goal Hierarchy Session: The student must learn how to envision and anticipate the necessary sub-goals or steps in the goal-setting process. With help the student can begin by selecting a possible goal and creating a hierarchy of the most likely steps in a plan or goal strategy. The adolescent continues to work with interested others in making the transition from indifference to goal planning in a friendly context.

It is not the purpose of this program to guarantee that all students finalize their goals or goal plans. The purpose is that students engage in the progress of moving towards goal fulfillment and cognitive development. The results of applying selective attention needs to reflect some learning improvement ongoing before there will be expenditures of effort (perseverance). Students should show and be "rewarded" for their progress in the project. When effort begins to have some pay offs in terms of educational progress positive feedback and support should follow. The student should become more motivated. The students should rehearse important points frequently. This rehearsal or redundancy helps to establish brain pathways for creative thinking.

Progress evaluation. There should be some practical built-in markers indicating where the adolescent is, on route to a goal. These markers could include: grade improvements, better choice of relevant courses, continual advisement from staff, gaining more information about goal content and better thinking about the future. There should be a consistency in the program, an increase in goal sources, supporters, and homework time. The adolescent should be equipped to measure his own progress. He should be able to see an improvement in his personal sense of well-being. The process of setting sub goals leads into the process of reorganizing the self. Cognitive change and life changes both result from personal perceptions.

At the same time, the adolescent gets an opportunity to refine his own views on well-being and held values. He or she is then able to incorporate personal values into a developing sense of commitment and success. This leads right into a motivated life. The motivated life consists of an on-going pattern of conflicting sub steps on a gradual basis.

How will I know when I am there? The adolescent will maintain a personal log of his journey. The log will start out with personal assessments of his beginning and progress at each step. The student will be able to compare his initial desires, feelings, and goals to where he is at any given point, although desires, feelings, and goals can and will change. Personal values will become more meaningful and less reactive to negative circumstances. The adolescent is ready to make the needed adjustments to achieve. When the adolescent has taken significant steps on a motivational journey, he has already achieved specific results. There is no possible evaluation or feedback without action. Writing down progress steps is in itself motivational and therapeutic.

The duration of the adolescents' goal pursuit cannot be precisely predicted. But target dates to complete certain activities or levels of mastery can be projected. For example: completing courses successfully; having a satisfactory performance level in a given program; getting involved researching a given topic or people in a given field of interest; attaining a diploma that prepares the student for something relating to a goal beyond getting out of high school.

The student should have accomplished specific requirements for qualification to a specific field of study or occupation.

Program components. The motivational program includes three major assignments: reading, discussion, and urban site visitations. The reading assignment should be brief overviews so that the adolescent will not be intimidated or bogged down in unnecessary details. Yet the adolescent must begin to adopt reading as a personal means of growth. Reading enhances the level of perception and analysts. The instructor will introduce each reading assignment and pave the way for student interest and attention. The student will be required to read three short biographies, three short articles or booklets on three cities, and three booklets on three different occupations. The students may use the Internet. The overall purpose of the reading is to expand the perspective of these important subjects beyond the localized perspectives and train the mind to process the information. The choices are made by the facilitator.

The program is flexible in that one to three books or booklets can be used for any of the three subjects or topics (short biographies, contemporary cities, and occupations). The content of these reading assignments are as follows:

1. **Short biographies**: To examine people's lives from a wide perspective of events, activities, challenges, hardships, and struggles to discover the daily experiences that shape people's lives, attitudes, and accomplishments or failures; to examine the diverse strategies people choose in order to overcome personal and environmental obstacles; to examine the roles of the key players, the turning points in their lives, and the plot or main theme played out in the story; and to discover the network and relationship circle of the characters. The students should be exposed to different views of success and focused lives. The reading should be taken seriously in student planning for the future and for discussion. This also becomes at the same time a collective study on narratology with personal application.

2. **Occupations and Concepts**: To help the adolescent get an insider's view of what it means to engage in an occupation in some chosen field or domain of thinking. The occupations discussed in the program do not have to be the same ones chosen by the student. The purpose is to learn more about expected specific qualifications and the knowledge base required. Students should know what is meant by "thinking domains." The second part is to choose a related idea, concept or principle to analyze or break down through select attention. How do you take a scientific or technical principle and analyze it until you fully understand it? What is the concept behind balancing an equation, dealing with analytic geometry, cellular biology or economics? The student learns and uses the principle of executive (controlled) attention and information processing to increase understanding.

3. **Contemporary cities**: To examine the realities of urban life from a broad perspective. The adolescent needs to see how the various social institutions work to impact how people live in the cities. The tour can include transportation, law enforcement, banking, schools, businesses, and government. The tour aspect can be limited if that is more practical. Adolescents should come to realize the magnitude of a city/urban operation and the ideas that undergird these institutions. The students need to be aware of the complexity, inter-relationships, and regulatory aspects of urban life. The adolescent will at some point have to negotiate with these institutions. Institutions have a mind-set and social-global perspectives. Figure 2 life in society provide an overview of social interactions.

Following institutional walk-throughs, a follow-up group discussion needs to be held in order to point out the most relevant features of each place and topic. The student can ask himself the questions: Can I fit into this picture? If I do not feel I fit in, what reasons do I have for not fitting in? What would I like to do in this environment? If I had to profile myself in my social-educational environment what would it look like? Perhaps every student who attends these sessions should profile themselves in writing.

What is your circle (constellation) of relationships? How do they affect your life?

Skills in Development: Social Intelligence

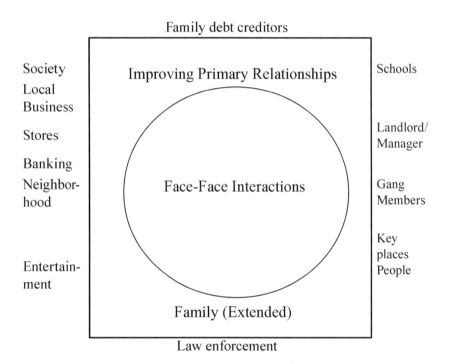

Family debt creditors

Society Local Business	Improving Primary Relationships	Schools

Stores — Landlord/Manager

Banking Neighbor-hood — Face-Face Interactions — Gang Members

Entertain-ment — Key places People

Family (Extended)

Law enforcement

Skills: as organizing principle:	Skills that develop perception Attention (focus) memory
Skills to bring to society	Skills that lead to success
Skills in preparation	Skills that help in school
Skills needed by employers	Skills that manage finance

Life in Society

How can you use the principle of effort, attention and information – processing to master the domain of your interest?

How can you devise a multi-facet approach to examining any subject as you prepare to broaden your knowledge base for success?

Everything is local. The quality of your local relationships helps to determine your future ability to expand to wider circles. Isolation from the real world limits your capacity to see things on bigger levels. You need a more complete picture of life. You will have social, economic, and educational hindrances that tend to reduce your effectiveness. Look ahead!

The Motivated Life: More Than a Dream

A revised understanding of motivational theory has helped to create a seven-step format from data present in the study. This information, along with the data, has helped to determine when goal setting was really taking place. It also helped to see motivation as a longitudinal (ongoing) process that defines how successful persons can maintain and improve their well-being and quality of life as they constantly face challenges.

Personal ideology as a set of related ideas was reflected in the adolescents as a value orientation. Value orientation and social perspectives on global life helps to take individuals out of their limited mental domain. Adolescents often seem to lack motivation but motivation is put in the service of social goals. Social goals are contextually dependent. Environments change slowly. Therefore, the situation for urban adolescents will change slowly if their localized social-political dynamics remain essentially unchanged.

In summation, the study provides a significant perspective on the many factors that link the social-culture, the individual and a goal-setting process. This relationship has not been fully developed in the literature. The study helps to show the impact of episodic events upon the lives of urban adolescents and their notions of success.

This investigation has demonstrated that qualitative data can be used to examine the impact of social markers upon the lives and goal setting of working-class adolescents. This includes quantitative date about their economic, social, and educational challenges. The composite effect of social indicators can be seen in a more direct way when the data is alive and responsive to interactive field investigation. Reality is seen in its immediate context. Success is seen as a social accomplishment in overcoming barriers to well-being and respect. Success in the study is more personal for those who identify less with global society. Success is not institutionalized. It is not tied into the functional roles of a structured society.

In another light, official state data on: local unemployment, job availability, school performance, crime statistics, health conditions, health care, noise levels, graduation rates, test scores, public recreation, after-school programs, and education related to the job market, complements the qualitative data on urban subjective experiences present in the local community. The study has shown that for those living under pressing conditions, the meaning of success tends to be different than it would be for those in the larger society. It tends to be more subjectively understood in light of a more problematic development process.

Finally, there is the psychological toil that exacerbates the conditions of marginalized living. People who live under constrictive conditions in at-risk environments experience the added stress of daily survival. The psychological well-being of the individual is jeopardized under chronic oppressive conditions (Oishi). When the individual feels he or she has little power or control over his or her life, his motivational efforts may be affected. This is why a long term approach must be built into the motivational life. The individual needs to seek more than the extrinsic rewards of socially approved occupations and educational attainment. Long-term goals should include autonomy, self-discipline, and keen observations in chosen domains. This is one reason why notions about success and academic performance may, in many cases, serve the need for well-being and confidence building in putting together a disciplined life. Academic goals do not exist in isolation, but are affected by contextual factors. Therefore people need more than academic goals in a fast track global world where academic rewards and occupational success might be short-lived. The unpredictable nature of the world-environment warns us that a motivated flexible life with long term vision must be cultivated.

The process of setting goals according to the data is a part of a gradual process of awakening. Conditions and feedback from family support and others help to shape individual goal thinking. The family, according to the literature, plays a major role in adolescent life whenever present. This was confirmed in the study. Goal setting is a social construction. For the adolescent, it emerges out of class, cultural perspectives, and social experience. The student must cope with forces beyond his or her scope in order to perform adequately in a rigid setting. He or she does not automatically adjust to social institutions not designed for the individual. Each step in the goal-setting process involves strong intentions and effort. The ability to think clearly, handle mainstream life, and relate to institutionalized learning may not be easy for those who are out of the social mainstream in the first place. This study is valuable because it helps to demonstrate the needs, challenges, and complexity of adolescent goal setting. It shows the other side of educational pursuit within the structural complex of society. This study does not examine personal motivation as if society does not exist. The individual cannot be separated from his immediate environment. The environment helps to describe who we are and why we do what we do in life. Environment creates conditions that help to develop certain life patterns and personality tendencies in people. Individuals respond to their life-space.

Future research should be able to use this study to further investigate contextual and awakening factors that encourage self-reflection and decision making in a complex environment. The role of both mainstream culture and adolescent culture should be studied in order to discover exactly what common factors can be used to create a process of relevant, meaningful goal pursuit in the community.

Structured Society

In regards to the plight and approaches to social achievement, urban education, and future well-being, the picture is still complex. It has to be complex because the wider context of global life can be misleading and complex. The needs and goals of global society, public education, political and economic structures are going to take precedence over the needs of any particular subculture or group. There will continue to be social inequalities in urban centers. Institutions also have their goals systems and future projections. In fact, institutions are goal structures in themselves. All institutions have their own visions and agendas. Schools are Bureaucracies with norms, a mind set, philosophies, ideologies with power and authority systems. This places a heavy mandate upon students, parents, and interested educators to become innovative and creative in meeting the needs and goals of people seeking to make the most out of their lives.

Goal-setting and goal-strategy planning are a must. Goal allies will have to partnership if possible with political sources, community, and well meaning institutions. Social-political structures and policymakers are objects of negotiation. This involves the old dilemma of individual autonomy interacting with inflexible social structures

The question emerges on how much can people help themselves when they are preoccupied with survival on a day-to-day basis? This paradox was clearly seen in the study. Are people able to think and process observations in a timely and rational manner?

Critical theory will continue to pursue full citizen participation in policy making, accessibility of resources and knowledge in society. Bandura has asserted, without the aggressive participation of concerned citizens in the institutional affairs of society the marginalized will get weaker and the social structures stronger and more deterministic.

Building the Motivated Life: From Reflection to Paths of Success

The reality of the motivated life comes into existence as a personal construction project. It is a seeking life. A combination of many factors contributes to its formation. The person becomes an object of personal managed care. This means the person is ready to measure, to assess his or her own life. The person has enough care and concern, faith and courage to move beyond a mediocre, barren life. The individual decides to include a working list of building blocks that lead to personal transformation and newness of being. The new you is the results of a motivated life. This includes a goal-state (an ongoing ideal) of a simple unentangled life-style. From adolescence into adulthood people must learn that they cannot afford to be chocked to death (barrenness) by the many social factors and unorganized tendencies that rob persons out of their dreams. People must learn to do that which really matters to them and the community. This takes thought and evaluation.

For example, we live in a demanding, over burdening world pulling us on every side of life. This causes us to experience a decentered self that has no control, focus or self-control. We feel "out of it". This experience is a part of the "post-modern age." Therefore, we need to pay more attention to our state of being. Do not neglect your transformed, transcendant state. This is a state that dwells on more ultimate matters for many this might be the spiritual side of their existence. But the realization is that we are more than flesh and blood. We are thinking, feeling expressive creatures who need a sense of meaning and well-being.

We learned in the study to: work by intentional steps, make better decisions, think long range, but act from day to day, consult with informed relational persons. Be sure to focus in particular domains that reinforce a higher level of thinking and ultimate concerns. Productive domains include: skill development, history, biographies, wisdom teaching, a personal belief system, trusted allies, time management, uplifting events, and experiences. Plasticity means you can change your thinking and expand your life. Do not imprison yourself with self-defeating ideas and negative people. Be a student all of your life. Create a new constellation of forward moving people and ideas – a new peer group if you will. Build a new reality. Possibility means your future is always open if you will seek it.

APPENDIX A
Definitions Related to the Study

Achievement –task motivation: A need-driven motive that becomes a cognitive schema or mind-set derived from social and cultural arousal. It is a goal state that orients and moves behavioral actions and dispositions. Persons develop achievement imagery over time. Goals of accomplishment, excellence, and strong anticipations involve overcoming problems, obstacles, and risks. Sometimes a measure of achievement is really a measure of the achievement motive and behavior. There is occupational- or career-oriented achievement and school-related achievement. The incentive for the achievement motive must satisfy the performer. The person needs performance feedback (McClelland).

Aspirations: Idealized images of future states. People have a need for inspired idealizations, which can come in the form of aspirations. People are often careless about making idealizations work. Idealizations and aspirations require self-regulation and application (Weissman).

The Black experience: The unique set of events, problems, and issues that have impacted people of African descent as an integral part of and in the context of broader American society. The reality of these experiences have often been lost or hidden in the mainstream of American life and history. African American participation in society has had a subordinated position in terms of value, legitimacy, and psychological and social perspective. Many of the defining features of African American participation have been emerged in Eurocentric proclivities presented as universal (Anderson).

Case study: A case is a specific, bounded particularistic system that focuses on a person, event, or institution as a single unit (Holliday). Case study provides more depth of information than a survey or questionnaire. The case exists in a particular environment and culture. The case study is less an exhaustive investigation about a subject but more about understanding information in regards to a key focus. It is not a method but a process involving diverse types of data combined to create a case. It is especially useful for multiphasic, explanatory research (Merriam; Yin).

Development: Changes that occur in a person's life over time. The model for this study involves the importance of the person in his or her environment. In this context, psychosocial issues of identity, conflicts, issues, values, ideals, autonomy, decision making, meaning-making ability, self-regulation ability, and increased perception emerge over time in the context of micro and macro (small and large) environments. The environment helps to determine paths, resources, and how values are shaped. Development and transformation are related in that in both changes include social, physical, and mental development. Transformation is the development of the inner structures of reflection, emotion, and social responsibility. It is the growth of basic attitudes and use of knowledge in life (Shaffer).

Goal setting: A personal striving. Goal setting involves task and expectancy-driven actions; it is to be in pursuit of or train toward a future. In goal settings, one engages in a self-imposed function for a desired future or outcome or an organized action for an anticipated reward (Carver & Scheier).

Ideology: A set of related ideas that are informed by a given knowledge base and past experience. This set of beliefs informs a worldview and interprets known events. These ideas are often connected to certain groups and circles (Adams & Sydie). Ideology is significant because it is an orientation and way of thinking which informs goals and goal-related activities. In a developmental sense, ideology becomes a psychic posture within the society that youth develop in over time (Gutek; Weissman).

Positionality: The self-understanding of a person's location in society in terms of identity, class, race, age, gender, and ideology (Banks; Freire).

Self-regulation: This item is used in regard to learning and goal setting. It refers to the act of planning, setting goals, finding goal pathways (strategies), and use of time and attention. This is a metacognitive process where the student thinks about his or her learning and planning actions (Ormrod).

Social context: An arena in which things exist. This includes power relationships, order, language, institutional forms, inequalities, technological state, ideas, and culture that impose upon people their experiences and identities (Wetherell).

Social structure: The ordering or framing of organizations, rules, regulations, ideologies, authority, and prestige that leads to a stable permanence. Social structures help produce social realities that shape how people live and think. Power is the social energy of structures which work to create or hinder practices and events (Lemert).

The set of ordered dynamic parts that invoke social and psychological reactions such as avoidance, opposition, and compliance (Radcliffe-Brown).

Transformation: Transformation deals with the holistic changes that occur in a person's life as a result of particular actions, pursuits and experiences. A sense of change, newness and make-over completes the felt identity of the person who is more prepared to engage the world on a better personal foundation.

Triangulation: Triangulation involves the use of multiple sources of data for study in order to increase the rigor and validity of the research (Yin).

Urban: Characteristic of the city and its regional geographic area that is comprised of condensed diverse populations, industry, economic activity, and competitive, dynamic commerce. Urban life is ordered by a particular kind of infrastructure, social and recreational life, political machinery, and heavy use of technology. In summation, urban life can be described by its complexity, diversity, and density (Mohl). Urban reality was first defined quantitatively, but more recently qualitative studies have begun to deal with gaps and problems of imprecise data, flawed methodology, and misinterpretations (Mohl).

Well-being: The satisfied mental and emotional state that enables a person to fully perform and set goals. Goal striving is the proactive route for developed vitality and psychosocial well-being. Well-being and goal setting are related (Sheldon et al.).

APPENDIX B
THE STUDY SET-UP

The Method of Discovery

This study was designed to deal with three areas of goal-setting: (1) motivational goals setting as a realistic tool for developing adolescents and young adults; (2) the social context and factors that affect the lives and motivation of persons living in urban areas; and (3) the particular motivational and learning tendencies of those who are reported to face the greatest challenges. Hopefully insights gained from the study will help all developing, striving persons to engage in the benefits of the motivational life. The study sought to investigate the experiences, thinking, and episodic events in adolescent life that could affect personal choices and goal-setting orientation of those in the study. There are many interwoven factors involved in the study. Individual, contextual, and academic data was used in the research. The research is designed to produce information and understanding, not to generalize a wider population.

Rationale for Qualitative Method

A research study requires an explanation of the phenomenon of interest and a reliable means to obtain the data sought. In this study, the explanation includes multiple factors in the investigative sequence. Together these factors, listed below, contribute to the rationale of the study:

- The expectation of success and well-being present in American society is unrealistic, difficult, and minimal without setting and pursuing goals.

- The literature shows that there are ongoing social-historical problems regarding African American urban male adolescent failures and underachievement that need attention.

- There are contextual or impacting environmental and personal factors that affect adolescent achievement, goals, and well-being, such as: schools, urban life, political realities, and motivational orientation. These interactive, interwoven factors are present at the same time.

- An investigation that has many interactive factors requires a method that can adequately explore these factors. In this study the method has to include an investigation of the social circumstances, perceptions, experiences, and personal motivational tendencies of urban Black male adolescents in their setting. The qualitative instrument is more appropriate for this study. The investigation should also lead to insights that can be used as a wider base for theory building.

Based upon multiple factors involved in the investigation and the research questions that flow out of these factors, I decided to conduct a qualitative rather than a quantitative study and move beyond numbers, charts and trends, although they are used in this study. In particular, open-ended interviews allow the research to deal with both concrete and abstract ideas through narrative sharing. Interviews reveal how the subject understands a piece of his or her world and responds to this perception. Adolescent perception informs the subject's motivational and goal-setting orientation.

In the past, motivational theory tended to focus upon constructs like mastery versus performance, ego versus task goals, attribution, extrinsic versus intrinsic orientation, single goals versus (recently) multiple-goal theory, and approach versus avoidance motivation (Weiner). But recently, there has been a proliferation of research and attention on achievement goals and related contextual issues. The perspective on goal theory has widened to include many factors, including life itself.

Goal-setting strategy is offered as one major approach for effectively dealing with the educational failures of urban adolescent males. Goal-setting strategy is based upon the application of a relevant goal-setting theory. This study focuses on four significant gaps that were found through a literature search. The four gaps include a sense of well-being, personal values, social goals, and futuristic anticipation of success. These topics of adolescent concerns were barely mentioned in the literature. Holistic understanding of adolescent motivation, including these gaps and contextual factors will help in goal-theory development.

The Subjects of Study

The research that was conducted focused on four under-studied factors identified through the literature review and how they play out in the urban context. The Adolescents came from a large comprehensive urban high school of 4,500. The students were interviewed. The school SAT scores were slightly higher than those at most of the general high schools in the area. At the same time 91 percent of the students were on some kind of public assistance. Most of the students were enrolled in the general, non-specialized program.

The grand tour question in this study is: To what degree, if any, do urban adolescent males engage in goal-setting activity?

Sub-questions:

- How do these adolescent males define success?

- If they set goals, how do the goals originate? What influences were present in the goal-setting process and the school experience of the adolescent? Was setting goals for the future important to them?

- Do the adolescents seek help in setting goals or learning about future options? Is help available from counselors, relatives, and library resources?

- Are the respondents willing to make personal adjustments in order to attain their goals? Pursuing goals includes the personal arrangements it takes to accomplish something.

- Are the adolescents easily discouraged in setting goals? Did they feel confident about setting goals? What were the hindrances present in setting goals and following through with them?

- What views do they have about school and society that may have affected the setting of goals? Do the adolescents feel they have adequate opportunities to achieve? What, if anything, did they do about the opportunities that were present?

A Consideration of Paradigms

Research begins with a view of the world and assumptions about reality. Views about the world inform our way of seeking to know more about the world (epistemological or knowledge approach). The investigator must begin with a view of the world that can help inform his or her search for accurate information about the world. In other words, the researcher relies upon his or her view of the world to inform his or her methodology. How people choose to see the world and gain information about the world can be put together as a logical collection of related assumptions and concepts. This includes perspectives and propositions about ways of knowing and measuring reality. A collection of related assumptions and models about reality in the world is called a paradigm.

Paradigms provide a sense of direction and order for the researcher; but paradigms may also be misleading, in that often hidden subjective reasoning and unquestioned assumptions go unchallenged (Patton). Epistemology deals with which approach is best in obtaining knowledge. My epistemological question is: Which approach is best for obtaining knowledge about the motivational goal-setting tendencies in African American urban male adolescents? In deciding the best way to obtain this knowledge, I asked some key questions:

1. What is the purpose of the research?
2. What kind of information am I looking for?
3. What possible methods will help provide the type of data needed?

The purpose of the research was to discover the process and the influences and factors that affect goal-setting tendencies in male urban adolescents. What values, experiences, and state of being (as well-being) affect futuristic anticipations of adolescent urban males? What method would help provide greater understanding of these factors? The information the study sought to obtain involved insights on interrelationships, themes, and perspectives as they are grounded in social activities and personal experience. Two approaches were considered in the process of deciding the most appropriate or relevant method of investigation. The study considered both the quantitative and qualitative means of investigation.

The Positivism Paradigm

A survey research method was initially considered. The survey method would have to operate under the assumptions of the positivistic paradigm. This paradigm assumes that there is one objective reality which can be known and precisely measured (quantified). A rational, to the point, quantitative approach seemed to provide answers to my inquiry, but my research question had many aspects and layers of possible meaning. The research question could not be answered through a short survey or summary questionnaire.

Jarvela states that the limitation of surveys is that you cannot load them down with too many factors. They should be used to study a few major variables. The nature of the survey method limits the focus of thinking and response of the respondent. In regards to laboratory experiments, the results do not always represent reality in the outside environment. Determining the social reality and academic orientation of high school adolescents was important for this study. Cokley points out that there are ethnic differences in the quantitative measurement of academic self-concept among groups. The nature of the scale factor/loadings used in questionnaires is different for White and Black adolescents. Further, the results are interpreted differently. For example, Black students use a wider context to evaluate their academic ability, not just school. These findings were not considered in most of the quantitative studies done in regards to Black academic self-concepts and educational orientation.

Another problem was that I could not find an instrument that precisely measured what I wanted, especially in light of the very recent changes and gaps in goal-setting theory. There are, however, many tests for tendencies such as attribution, competence, self-esteem, motives, aspirations, traits, need for achievement, incentives, and intrinsic versus extrinsic and mastery versus task orientation.

In this study, using interviews worked to bring personal and contextual factors together through the research questions.

The Qualitative Paradigm

Qualitative research involves a holistic approach. Qualitative research deals with a social world of many realities, meanings, and perspectives. The general umbrella term "qualitative research" could include ethnography, anthropology, phenomenology, case studies, and so on. It deals with naturalistic situations, in-depth data, empathetic neutrality, and inductive reasoning. This research also deals with contextual sensitivity and descriptive data. Reality is constructed and not a given. The researcher must be careful not to impose his or her thinking or feeling on research subjects and their perspectives. As the researcher's role is to discover the subject's reality, the researcher must be open and not judgmental. Rather than developing categories beforehand, data categories result from descriptive data, including unfolding patterns and concepts that emerge as the research proceeds. This role of discovery helps to promote openness in the research because the research cannot always predetermine exactly which factors are the critical factors in answering research questions. The question of goal setting and achievement in this study can lead to many possible answers or possible explanations.

Pilot Study

These students were a part of an after-school cultural center recreation program where the pilot interviews were held in the school district. The two students who were interviewed (one by me) were asked questions about their schools, life episodes, success, personal values, social views and personal efforts in goal-setting activity. The survey that involved 20 students focused only on their understanding of success. It was called a "success survey." The only question was about student views on success. Success is an important concept among African American youth (Fordham). Students selected for the pilot study involved a convenience sample rather than systematic selection process. The success survey showed clearly that the students did not view school academics as the means to success. Success was contextually and subjectively defined. This response caused me to look closely at the relationship of success, achievement, and goal setting. It was a major consideration for the study.

The success survey showed that the students understanding of success was discussed in terms of the adolescent's future well-being. The success survey reinforced the high value the students placed on the role of success. Success was based upon the student's need for social and economic accomplishment, not academic achievement.

The adolescents seemed to prefer a biographical narrative style of sharing rather than responding to a series of formal questions one at a time. During the biographic storytelling, many of the intended questions were answered before they were asked. The students interviewed responded to questions about success in terms of well-being and personal satisfaction and not in terms of academic or occupational achievement. The students appeared to have little awareness of possible occupations and their requirements, or what was available to them in the present job market. They seemed to struggle at possible goal choices when asked. The students reported that their history in school prior to high school was largely uneventful and non-stimulating.

Great effect was made to allow the interview to go where the students wanted it to go and still get the necessary data. The students reported that few people had affected their future interest or goals in anything.

The Research Design: The "Case" as a Strategy of Study

The main method that was used in this study to obtain information was individual in-person interviews. Each student in the study became a unit of study. In addition to interview data, other related information was also obtained about the school, the neighborhood, and the city. All of this information together formed a composite description of the study unit, the student—the urban adolescent. In this light, the study became more than interviews: it became a case study centered around an empirical question on motivational tendencies. An understanding of motivation goal-setting and cognition in the study was derived from scientific inquiry. That is the process of investigation was clearly designed according to related concepts and procedures. The student is seen in a more holistic light with many factors converging together. Merriam reported from his own research that a case study is an end product resulting from a holistic exploratory description. The end results become a case when integrated particularistic data is obtained from multiple sources. The entire setting, including the context (field) and its main components, produces a case study. In this study the investigation is really about motivational tendencies of a test group. Empirical questions are being addressed in a cognitive study in a contextual environment.

The case study is a strategy used in an empirical investigation of a particular unit of observation using multiple sources of evidence within a real-life context. Information about each person in the study comes together to form a composite picture about that individual. A case study approach aims to explore, describe, understand, and interpret diverse information gained through interviews and other data. It is not an exhaustive study of the subject but the utilization of a number of sources gathered around a major point—the objective of the study. It is a process of study around a particular bounded unit (Holliday). The study transcends the notion of a simplistic investigation/observation of a single level inquiry.

Case study strategy involves select samples, concepts, questions, self-reporting, and contextual data. The purpose of the data is to provide new or added levels of awareness, information for decision making, or discovery of overlooked patterns and concepts. Case study is a phenomenon in context. It has been viewed by some researchers in the past as plain and non-challenging. But when examined in more diverse detail case study can be scientifically challenging. It is a creative process involving many sources of data. It is a way of looking at the combination of certain experiences occurring in similar units. For example, this study involved data on student performance, neighborhoods, culture, city schools, employment, and academic test results. This investigation is centered upon related information on goal-setting and motivational studies.

The advantages of the case study process are:

- Case study takes the researcher into settings where he or she may not have gone if the information were readily available in another form.

- The researcher might have to visit different neighborhoods, schools, or communities in order to obtain information firsthand. In other words, the study follows the case.

- Case study exposes the researcher to different cultures, languages, capital, and people who offer a different view and perspective on life in their world. Another side of reality is made available.

- Case study involves various kinds of data gathering such as archival, statistical reports and demographic information (Yin).

- Case study helps to facilitate the application of theory thinking to real-life situations. Theory thinking is not done in isolation.

- Case study helps the researcher to view the object of investigation from a holistic perspective. This includes the complexity, heuristic (problem-solving) nuances and contextual episodes that affect the thinking and behavior of the object of study.

- Case study can include phenomenal storytelling or biographical narrative.

- People tend to think about their lives and related meaning as stories

- (Atkinson). These stories contain a worldview, goals, psychological postures, the unfolding of surrounding relationships. The defining social role of the teller in his or her social order emerges in dialogue. The person depicts him- or herself in certain kinds of ways.

What ends up as a "case" is particularly useful when the context of the individual studied is interrelated with the social environment. The study method moves beyond fixed anticipated knowledge to the realm of real investigation, exploration, and discovery. The attention of the researcher is so flexible and responsive it can be refocused during the investigation, as the subject expresses felt meaning and life events. The study allows contextual data to provide meaningful knowledge about the subject. The social order in which the subjects exist is what makes them describable, explainable, and predictable (Smedslund). Behaviors make more sense when viewed from a specific social order that informs the "rationale" of thinking and behavior.

Qualitative study can also shed light on unclear statistical correlations from other studies (Freeman, Gutman, & Midgley). The subjects themselves can give their own reports about casual factors in their own lives. Another advantage is that there are no deliberate manipulations or experimental acts by the interviewer. The subject engages in the act of self-disclosure without pressure. The subject can choose how he or she wants to deal with any question. The strength of the study is that it can deal with many factors and is grounded in the self-constructed reality of the subject. Way argues that she used the case study interview method with Black urban adolescent males because it is a voice-centered method that allows human voices, stories and feelings to be heard in cases involving complex thoughts and emotion. The contrast of the other "voice" can shed light on the typical voices we are used to hearing.

McAdams states that human storytelling is the most natural means of research. This is why there has been a strong upsurge of interest in psychological studies using life stories and personal narrative methods. Erik Erikson the great identity psychologist did work on psychohistory narratives many years ago (1950-1973). The narrative life-mind unfolds personal meaning, experience, and social processes. The storyteller makes sense of his or her own reflective life. Storytelling presupposes a sense of self. There is deeper data involved in the act of investigative inquiry of storytelling than some other methods of study. Narrations are oral and conceptual statements projecting an experienced reality.

Ragin reports that the most valuable aspect of interview studies is that they can provide an extensive dialogue between the ideas of the researcher and the responding case. The play on ideas and meaningful, real exchange is in itself a great empirical and intellectual phenomenon. The investigator approaches case study with meaningful questions in hopes that rich data will result from the idea of evidence dialogue.

The weaknesses and challenges of the interview method and case study are (1) to allow the data to speak without imposition; (2) to avoid over generalizing the information; and (3) to ensure honesty in self-reporting since the purpose of all research is to explain and interpret in a truthful and accurate manner. This means that all the data should be subject to accurate assessment, interpretation and explanation.

A case unit involves the holistic gathering of related information centered around specific interest issues and concerns. In this study the task is exploring goal-setting orientation among adolescents in the urban environment. The process of investigating "a case" helps to draw out of the study information for a wider understanding of meaning, concepts, and happenings in the larger social context.

Study Population and Sampling Methods

A review of the literature provides a suggestive method for subject selection for case studies. The goal of the study is to deal with understanding and discovery, not prediction and hypothesis testing. The subjects are chosen to provide adequate data to support the study. They should represent the group and settings of interest. This is intentional sampling. The focus of this study is "the typical" Black urban male adolescent. The typical Black male adolescent is not in an honors high school, nor in an honors classification. He is not a dropout and he is not consistently a behavioral problem. The chosen adolescents live in a working-class urban neighborhood.

The Interview Exchange

The interview is usually the main road to research dealing with multiple realities (Stake). People make themselves available to each other during interviews. Interviews are valuable in that they provide a means of seeing how the societal structures impact upon the routine life of the subject.

Interviews were based upon the assumption that the study was dealing with active, informed respondents who were practitioners of a particular form of life. Interviews were crafted with the aim of participating in the existential reality of the subject. Each interview was unique and not a copy of another. Each student was viewed as a separate but related individual. The adolescent in this study was treated as an equal partner in the investigative process. The student had a demonstrated claim on a repository of information desired by the interviewer. The interviews were aimed at capturing a life profile description and overview of the adolescent's school-related and goal-related activities. Questions were centered upon the feelings and experiences of the adolescent in order to ascertain his reflections about well-being, the future, goal-setting tendencies, and sense of personal values. The interviews were not designed to create a detailed biography. It was the purpose of the interviews to investigate and understand the educational journey of the adolescent. The role of the interviewer was to listen and serve as a guide.

Quantitative researchers sharply define everything first and look for "fits" afterward; in qualitative interviews, the respondent answers questions at his or her own ease and ability. The subjects in this study determined the pace of the interviews and particular areas of major interest. The study encouraged free-flowing narrative data that accurately reflected the thoughts of the respondent. The interview was a guided conversation event. Interview results were obtained by accurately using student statements to arrive at research conclusions. Means to address interview validity are described below.

The subjects were told they were participating in an educationally centered interview. There was no deception used in the interviews. The students were accepted as partners in the research process. No real names were used for the interviews. The first three interviews were recorded, but the students did not seem too receptive about looking at recording devices so their use was discontinued. Merriam maintains that mechanical recording devices can be seen as obtrusive, especially for sensitive groups, in this surveillance climate of mistrust and suspicion. Merriam also contends that differences in age, gender or class can work the reverse effect in gaining trust. Sometimes interviewees relate to outsiders better than those who have some distance between them. This distance can produce feelings of increased objectivity and non intrusion between the subject and his or her interviewer. Having a "peer" doing the interviews is not necessarily trust producing. The subjects themselves have to determine what group, category, gender or age the effective interviewer should be.

Bryman argues that the test of case study reliability and validity can be approached by asking certain questions:

1. Is there a good match between the researcher's observations and the ideas that follow or are developed?
2. Can others closely replicate the study (reliability)?
3. Does the study appear credible (face validity)?
4. Is the written source of respondents' answers dependable and accurately recorded?

In regards to case interview reliability and validity, Huberman and Miles argue that multiple case sampling adds confidence to the findings. Merriam reports that validity is increased with the use of narrative vignettes of daily life that coincide with the general data. Berg claims that having multiple interviews also increase validity. Berg also states that the interviewer should say to the interviewee that he or she is an inquirer not an expert. In this study the interviewers presented themselves as seekers of information that would help others in their educational pursuits. This built rapport and increased the validity of the interview responses. The interviewer merely assisted the interviewees in conveying as much information as possible about the given subject. The interviewer provided accurate citations from the interview. The interviewers are not just interested in data; he or she is interested in discovery and in the subjects themselves.

Yin states that in order to increase the validity of a case study, the research design should include diverse sources of data. In this case they included: city and county records, interactions with some of the school staff, counselors, and contact persons on the school site. The study sought to find out about the role and policies of the school staff and the challenges they faced with entering students. These sources also helped to provide the methodological "triangulation" that was needed to increase study validity from many sources.

The following tables reflect the interviews conducted by the research assistant. The next table lists the participants in the study by age, grade average, and study program. There were 18 students who were a part of the regular testing and 2 who were pilot study students. The average GPA for the 18 students was 76.5 percent. This does not take into account the differences in the level of difficulty for the various programs. Most of the students in the survey (61 percent) were enrolled in the general studies program. Four students in the study out of 18 (27.7 percent) were enrolled in the college program. One student in the pilot study was enrolled in the college program. Enrollment in the college program does not necessarily mean the students are excelling. Enrollment in the college program varies from year to year. The ages ranged from 14 to 16. All high school grades, from 9 to 12, were included in the study.

Table 1

Research Assistant Summary

	Number of students
Pilot interviews	2
Study interviews	18
Research assistant: Complete interviews	3
Research assistant: Hip-hop interviews	5
Success Session (Neighborhood Adolescents)	20

Pilot student interviews were convenience samples. They are listed separately from the test high school adolescents.

Table 2

Adolescent Interview Listing, Names are Pseudonyms

Name	Case #	Age	Grade	GPA	Program
Byzan	1	16	11	87	General Studies
Bordan	2	16	10	80	General Studies
Eston	3	17	11	65	General Studies
Monk	4	17	11	78	General— Research Assistant
Rhad	5	17	12	80	General Studies
Fason	6	16	11	80	College— Research Assistant
Tyson	7	15	10	77	General Studies
Swan	8	17	12	77	General Studies
William	9	18	12	68	General— Research Assistant
Peterson	10	17	12	80	College
Oban	11	16	11	70	College
Themos	12	15	10	69	General Studies
Emil	13	17	12	69	General Studies

Balwin	14	18	12	70	General—Research Assistant
Gary	15	17	11	70	College—Research Assistant
Pinnock	16	14	9	95	College
Iane	17	14	9	74	Public Service/ROTC
Conroy	18	14	9	88	College
Barry	Pilot 1	16	11	70	College (Probation)
Carlin	Pilot 2	16	10	70	General—Research Assistant

The narratives of each respondent were treated as a reconstruction of the remembered lives of the adolescents. Each adolescent shared his own life perspective. The interviewer paid particular attention to episodic events, personal challenges, and pragmatic assessments reported by the students.

Data from the interviews were contrasted with information and views provided by the school staff and school program. The adolescents and the counselors both reported their positions or feelings about the expected role of the school and the students. This information was valuable in understanding the impact of school policies and approaches upon the goal-setting tendencies of Black male students.

Critical theory was utilized in that it was useful in examining power relationships, marginality, parents' ability to negotiate school structures, and the effects of social perspectives and policies upon people living in urban areas.

This study engages a real problem in the contemporary world. It relates social, psychological, and educational concepts in a holistic manner. The study can provide insights for those who are interested in addressing an educational and social dilemma of adolescents living and struggling in urban America.

REFERENCES

Adams, B., & Sydie, R. A. (2001). *Sociological theory.* Thousand Oaks: Pine Forge Press.

Allen, L., & Mitchell, C. (1998). Social and ethnic differences in patterns of problematic and adaptive development: An epidemiological review. In V. McLloyd & L. Steinberg (Eds.), *Studying minority adolescents* (pp. 29–54). Mahwah, NJ: Lawrence Erlbaum Assoc.

Allen, R. (2001). *The concept of self: A study of Black identity and self-esteem.* Detroit: Wayne State University Press.

Amen, Daniel (2008). Magnificent mind at any age. New York, Three Rivers Press.

Anderson, E. (1990). *Street wise.* Chicago: University of Chicago Press.

Anderson, T. (1990). *Black studies.* Pullman: Washington State University Press.

Anyon, J. (1997). *Ghetto schooling.* New York: Teacher's College Press

Arnett, J. J. (2001). *Adolescence and emerging adulthood.* Upper Saddle River: Prentice Hall.

Atkinson, T. P., & Coffey, A. (2001). Revisiting the relationship between participant observations and interviewing. In J. Gubrium & J. Holstein (Eds.), *Handbook of interview research* (pp. 801–814). Thousand Oaks: Sage.

Atkinson, R. (2001). The life story interview. In J. Gubrium & J. Holsein (Eds.), *Handbook of Interview Research.* (pp. 121–140). Thousand Oaks: Sage.

Bandura, A. (1997). *Self-efficacy, the exercise of control.* New York: W. H. Freeman.

Banks, J. (1996). The Canon debate, knowledge construction, and multicultural education. In J. Banks (Ed.), *Multicultural education, transformative knowledge, and action* (pp. 3–29). New York: Teachers College Press.

Bargh, J., & Gollwitzer, P. (1994). Environmental control of goal-directed action: Automatic and strategic contingencies between situations and behavior. In W. D. Spaulding (Ed.), *Nebraska symposium on motivation: Vol. 41. Integrative views of motivation, cognition, and emotion* (pp. 71–124). Lincoln: University of Nebraska Press.

Beck, R. C. (2000). *Motivation theories and principles.* Upper Saddle River: Prentice Hall.

Berg, S. (2007). *Qualitative research methods for the social sciences.* Boston: Pearson.

Boger, J. (1996). Race and the American city: The Kerner Commission Report in retrospect. In J. C. Boger & J. W. Wegner (Eds.), *Race, poverty, and American cities* (pp. 3–78). Chapel Hill: University of North Carolina Press.

Brides, L. (2003). *Coping as an element of developmental well-being.* In well-being M. Bornstein, L. Davidson, C. Keyes, & K. Moore (Eds.), (pp. 155–166). Mahwah: Lawrence Erlbaum Associates

Bryman, A. (2001). *Social research methods.* Oxford: Oxford University Press

Cantor, N., & Fleeson, W. (1994). Social intelligence and intelligent goal pursuit: A cognitive slice of motivation. In W. D. Spaulding (Ed.), *Nebraska symposium on motivation: Vol. 41. Integrative views of motivation cognition and emotion* (pp. 125–180). Lincoln: University of Nebraska Press.

Caprara, G., & Cervone, D. (2000). *Personality.* Cambridge: Cambridge University Press.

Carr, S., & MacLachlan, M. (1997). *Motivational Gravity In motivation and culture.* D. Munro, J. Schumaker, & S. Carr (Eds.). New York: Routledge.

Carter, C. (1995). *Majoring in high school.* New York: New York Press.

Carver, C. S., & Scheier, M. (1998). *On the self-regulation of behavior.* Cambridge: Cambridge University Press.

Carver, C. S., & Scheier, M. (1999). Stress, coping and self-regulatory processes. In L. A. Pervin & O. P. John (Eds.), *Handbook of Personality* (pp. 553–575). New York: Guilford Press.

Charles, M. (2002). Patterns building blocks of experience. New York: Routledge.

Cokley, K. (2003). What do we know about the motivation of African American students? Challenging the anti-intellectual myth. *Harvard Educational Review, 73*(4), 524-558.

Collins, P. (2006). *From Black power to hip-hop*. Philadelphia: Temple University Press.

Cornell, S., & Hartmann, D. (1998). *Ethnicity and race*. Thousand Oaks: Pine Forge Press.

Covington, M. (2000). Goal theory, motivation and school achievement: An integrative review. *Annual Review of Psychology, 51,* 171–200.

Cranton, P. (1994). *Understanding and promoting transformative learning*. San Francisco: Jossey-Bass.

Csikszentmihalyi, M., & Rathunde. (1993). The measurement of flow in everyday life: Toward a theory of emergent motivation. In J. Jacobs (Ed.), *Development perspectives in motivation* (pp 57–98). Lincoln University of Nebraska Press

Cuomo, A. (1998). *The state of the cities*. Washington, DC: U.S. Department of Housing and Urban Development.

Davidson, L., Rosenberg, M., & Moore, K. (2003) Well-being and the future: Using science based knowledge to inform practice and policy in well-being. M. Bornstein, L. Davidson, C. Keyes, and K. Moore (Eds.), *Well-being: Positive development across the life course* (pp 525-542) Mahwah: Lawrence Erlbaum Associates.

Dawson, M. (2001). *Black visions*. Chicago: University of Chicago Press.

Dienert, E. & Suh, E. (2000). Measuring subjective well-being to compare the quality of life of cultures. In E. Diener and E. Suh (Eds.), *Culture and subjective well-being* (pp 3-12) Cambridge: The MIT Press.

Doidge, N. (2007). *The brain that changes itself*. New York: Viking.

Downey, D., & Ainsworth-Damell, J. (2002, February). The search for oppositional culture among Black students. *American Sociologic Review,* 67(1), 156–164.

Eccles, J., & Wigfield, A. (2002). Motivational beliefs, values, and goals. *Annual Review of Psychology, 53,* 109–132.

Elliott, A. & Thrasher, T. (2001). Achievement goals and the hierarchical model of achievement motivation. *Educational Psychology Review.* 13.2, pp. 139-156

Ekstrom, L. (1993). A coherence theory of autonomy. *Philosophy and Phenomenological Research, 53*(3).

Emmons, R. (1996). Striving and feeling, personal goals and subjection. In P. Gollwitzer and J. Bargh (Eds.), *Well-being in the psychology of action* (pp. 313–337). New York: Guilford Press.

Emmons, R. A. & Kaiser, H. A. (1996). Goal orientation and emotional well-being linking goals and affect through the self. In L. Martin and A. Tesser (Eds.), *Striving and feeling, interactions among goals, affect and self regulation* (pp. 79–98). Mahwah, NJ: Lawrence Erlbaum.

Erikson, E. H. (1968). *Identity, youth and crisis.* New York: W. W. Norton.

Farkas, C., Lleras, C., & Maczuga, S. (2002). The search for oppositional culture among Black students. *American Sociological Review,* 67(1), 148–155.

Fordham, S. (1996). *Blacked out.* Chicago: University of Chicago Press.

Frankfort-Nachmias, E., & Nachmias, D. (1996). *Research methods in the social sciences.* New York: St. Martin's.

Franklin, J., & Moss, A., Jr. (1994). *From slavery to freedom.* New York: McGraw Hill.

Freeman, K., Gutman, L., & Midgley, C. (2002). Can achievement goal theory enhance our understanding of motivation and performance of African American young adolescents? In C. Midgley (Ed.), *Goals* (pp. 175–203). Mahwah, N.J.: Lawrence Erlbaum.

Freire, P. (1970). *Pedagogy of the oppressed.* New York: Continuum.

Giddens, A. (1984). *The constitution of society.* Berkeley: University of California Press.

Gmelch, G., & Zenner, W. eds. (2002). *Urban life: Readings in Urban Anthropology.* Prospect Heights, Ill.: Waveland

Goldfield, Abbot, Anderson, Argersinger, Argersinger, Barney, & Weir (2001). *The American journey,* vol. 2. Upper Saddle River: Prentice Hall.

Gollwitzer, P. (1996). The volitional benefits of planning. In P. Gollwitzer & J. Bargh (Eds.), *The psychology of action* (pp. 287–312). New York: Guilford Press.

Graham, S. (1994). Motivation in African Americans. *Review of Education, 4*(1), 55–116.

Graham, S. (1995). Narrative versus meta-analytic reviews of race references in motivation: A comment on Cooper and Dorn. *Review of Educational Research, 65*(4), 509–514.

Graham, S. (1996). What's "emotional" about social motivation? In J. Juvonen & K. Wentzel (Eds.), *Social motivation* (pp.346–360). Cambridge: Cambridge University Press.

Graham, S. (1997). Using attribution theory to understand social and academic motivation in African American youth. *Educational Psychologist 32*(1). 21-34.

Graham, S. (2001). Inferences about responsibility and values: Implication for academic motivation. In F. Salili, C. Chiu, & Y. Hong (Eds.), *Student motivation* (pp. 31–59). New York: Academic Press.

Grossberg, L. (1994). Introduction: Bring it all back home pedagogy and cultural studies. In *Between borders*. Eds. H. Giroux & P. McLaren (pp. 1–28). New York: Routledge.

Gutek, G. (1997). *Philosophical and ideological perspectives on education.* Boston: Allyn & Bacon.

Harter, S. (1993). Visions of self: Beyond the me in the mirror. In J. Jacobs (Ed.), *Developmental perspectives on motivation* (pp. 99–144). Lincoln: University of Nebraska Press.

Harrison, A., Wilson, M., Pine, C., Chan, S., & Buriel, R. (1990). Family ecologies of ethnic minority children. *Child Development, 61,* 347–362.

Healy, J. (1990). Endangered Minds. New York: Touchstone.

Henderson, V., & Dweck, C. (1990). Motivation and achievement. In S. Feldman & G. Elliott (Eds.), *At the threshold: The developing adolescent* (pp. 308–329). Cambridge: Harvard University Press.

Hettema, P. (1979) Personality and adaption. Amsterdam: Norm-Holland Publishing.

Hickey, D., & McCaslin, M. (2001). A Comparative, Socio cultural analysis of context and motivation In Motivation in learning contexts. S. Volet and S. Jarvela (Eds.), (pp. 33-56). Amsterdam: Pergamon.

Hitlin, S. (2003). Values as the core of personal identity: Drawing links between two theories of self. *Social Psychology Quarterly 66*(2), 118–137.

Holliday, A. (2002). *Doing and writing qualitative research.* Thousand Oaks: Sage.

Holzer, H., & Offner, P. (2004). *Forgotten men: the continuing crisis in Black male unemployment, and how to remedy it,* The American Prospect, pp.

Huberman, A., & Miles, M. (1994). Data management and analysis methods. In N. Denzin & Y. Lincoln (Eds), *Handbook of qualitative research* (pp. 236–247). Thousand Oaks: Sage.

Husman, J. & Lens, W. (1999). The role of the future in student motivation. *Educational Psychologist 34*(2), 113–125.

Jarvela, S. (2001). Shifting research on motivation and cognition to an integrated approach on learning and motivation in context. In S. Volet & S. Jarvela, *Motivation in learning contexts* (pp. 3–16). New York: Pergamon.

Jarvela, S., & Markku, N. (2001). Motivation in context: Challenges and possibilities in studying the role of motivation. In S. Volet & S. Jarvela (Eds.), *New pedagogical cultures in motivation in learning contexts* (pp. 105–128). Amsterdam: Pergamon.

Jarvis, P. (2006). Towards a comprehensive theory of human learning. London: Rutledge.

Jenkins, A. H. (1995). *Psychology and African Americans.* Boston: Allyn & Bacon.

Jensen, E. (2006). Enriching the brain. San Francisco: John Wiley & Sons.

Jones, J. (1988). Cultural differences in temporal perspectives: Instrumental and expressive behaviors in time. In J. McGrath (Ed.), *The social psychology of time* (pp. 21–38). Newbury Park: Sage.

Kaplan, A., & Maehr, M. L. (1999). Enhancing the motivation of African American students: An achievement goal theory. *The Journal of Negro Education, 68,* 23–41

Kellogg, R. (2007). Fundamentals of Cognitive Psychology.

Kerbo, H. (2003). *Social stratification and inequality.* Boston: McGraw Hill.

Kerckhoff, A. (2002). The transition from school to work. In J. Mortimer & R. Larson (Eds.), *The changing adolescent experience* (pp. 52–87). Cambridge: Cambridge University Press.

King, R., Stansfield, W. & Mulligan, P. (2006). A Dictionary of Genetics, Seventh Edition. Oxford, Oxford University Press.

Kirby, G. & Goodpaster, R. (2007) Thinking. Upper Saddle River, Pearson/Prentice Hall.

Kitwana, B. (2005). *Why White kids love hip-hop.* New York: Basic Civitas Books.

Kleniewski, N. (1997). *Cities, change and conflict.* Belmont: Wadsworth.

Knight, G., & Hill, N. (1998). Measurement equivalence in research involving minority adolescents. In V. McLloyd & L. Steinberg

(Eds.), *Studying minority adolescents* (pp. 183–210). Mahwah, NJ: Lawrence Erlbaum.

Kruglanski, A. (1996). Goals as knowledge structures. In P. Gollwitzer & J. Bargh (Eds.), *The psychology of action* (pp. 599–618). New York: Guilford.

Kuper, A. (1999). Culture. Cambridge: Howard University Press.

Leary, M., & Kowalski, R. (1995). *Social anxiety.* New York: Guilford Press.

LeCourt, D. (2004). *Identity matters.* Albany: State University of New York Press.

Leek, C. (2005). Semantic Memory Impairment: What can connectionist simulations reveal about the organization of conceptual knowledge. (Ed.), George Houghton I*n connectionist models in cognitive psychology.* New York: Psychology Press.

Lemert, C. (2002). *Social things.* Lanham: Rowman and Littlefield.

Letendre, G. (2000). *Learning to be adolescent.* New Haven: Yale University Press.

Lightfoot, Cynthia. (1997). *The culture of adolescent risk-taking.* New York: Guilford.

Lipman, P. (1998). *Race, class, and power in school restructuring.* Albany: State University of New York Press.

Long, R. (2005). *Motivation.* London: Fishbooks.

Lynch, G. and Granger, R. (2008). *Big Brain.* New York: Palgrave McMillian.

MacDonald, G., Saltzman, J. L., & Leary, M. R. (2003). Social approval and trait self-esteem. *Journal of Research in Personality, 37,* 23–40.

Marcus, H., Kitayama, S., & Heiman, R. (1996). Culture and basic psychological principles. In E. T. Higgins & A. W. Kruglanski (Eds.), *Social psychology* (pp. 857–913). New York: Guilford.

Marsick, V. J. (1998, Fall). Transformative learning from experience in the knowledge era, *Daedalus, 127*(4), 119-136.

Massey, D., & Denton, N. (1993). *American apartheid.* Cambridge: Harvard University Press

McAdams, D. (1999). Personal narratives and the life story. In L. Pervin & O. John (Eds), *Handbook of personality* (pp. 478–500). New York: Guilford.

McCaslin, M. & DiMarino-Linnen (2000). Motivation and learning in school: Societal contexts, psychological constructs, and educational practices. In *American education: Yesterday, today and tomorrow.* (Ed.) T. L. Good (pp. 84-151) Chicago: University of Chicago Press.

McClelland, D. (1970). Toward the theory of motive acquisition. In M. Miles & W. Charters, Jr. (Eds.), *Learning in social settings* (pp. 414–435). Boston: Allyn & Bacon.

McClelland, D. (1987). *Human motivation.* New York: Cambridge University Press.

McCollom, M. (1995). Re-evaluating group development: A critique of the familiar models. In J. Gillette & M. McCollom (Eds.), *Groups in context* (pp. 122–154). Lanham: University Press of America.

Merriam, S. (1998). *Qualitative research and case study applications in education.* San Francisco: Jossey-Bass.

Miller, A. (1993). Social science, social policy and the heritage of African-American families. In M. Katz (Ed.), *The "underclass" debate* (pp. 254-291). Princeton: Princeton University Press.

Mohl, R. (1997). New perspectives on American urban history. In R. Mohl (Ed.), *The making of urban America* (pp. 335–374). Wilmington: SR Books.

Mook, D. G. (1987). *Motivation, the organization of action.* New York: W. W. Norton.

Moshman, D. (1999). *Adolescent psychological development.* Mahwah, NJ: Lawrence Erlbaum.

Muss, R. E. (1996). *Theories of adolescence.* New York: McGraw-Hill.

Myrdal, G. (1996). *An American dilemma: The Negro problem and modern democracy.* New Brunswick: Transaction Publishers.

National Research Council (1993). *Losing generations.* Washington, DC: National Academy Press.

Nisbett, R. & Pervin P. (1977). The social bond. New York: Knopf.

Nisbett, R. (2009). Intelligence and How to Get It. New York, W. W. Norton & Company.

Nurmi, J., & Salmela-Aro, K. (2002). Goal construction and depressive symptoms in a life-span context: The transition from school to work. *Journal of Personality, 70*(3), 385-420.

Oehingen, G., & Gollwitzer. (2004). Goal setting and goal striving. In M. Brewer & M. Hewston (Eds.), *Emotion and motivation* (pp. 165–183). Oxford: Blackwell.

Offer, D., Ostrov, E., & Howard, K. (1981). *The adolescent.* New York: Basic Books.

Ogbu, J. (1997). African American education: A cultural-ecological perspective. In H. P. McAdoo (Ed.), *Black families* (pp. 234-250). Thousand Oaks: Sage.

Oishi, S. (2000). Goals as cornerstones of subjective well-being: Linking individuals and cultures. In Ed Diener and E. Sub (Eds.), *Culture and subjective well-being* (pp 87–112). Cambridge: MIT Press.

Oliver, R., & Leffel, T. (2006). *Hip-hop Inc.* New York: Thunder's Mouth.

Ormrod, J. (2003). *Educational psychology: Developing learners.* Upper Saddle River: Merrill Prentice Hall.

O'Sullivan, E. (1999). *Transformative learning.* Toronto: University of Toronto Press.

Oxford, J. (1992). *Community psychology: Theory and practice.* New York: John Wiley and Sons.

Parham, T., White, J., & Ajamu, A. (1999). *The psychology of Blacks: An African centered perspective.* Upper Saddle River: Prentice Hall.

Paster, V. (1994). The psychosocial development and coping of Black male adolescents: Clinical implications. In R. Majors & J. Gordon (Eds.), *The American Black male* (pp. 215-230). Chicago: Nelson-Hall.

Patton, M. (2003). *Qualitative research and evaluation methods.* Thousand Oaks: Sage.

Perls, F. (1969). Gestalt Therapy Vervbatim. New York: Bantam.

Perry, T., Steele, C., and Hilliard, A. (2003). *Young, gifted and Black.* Boston: Beacon Press.

Phinney, J., & Landin, J. (1998). Research paradigms for studying ethnic minority families within and across groups. In V. McLloyd & L. Steinberg (Eds.), *Studying minority adolescents: Conceptual, methodological, and theoretical issues* (pp. 89–10). Mahwah, NJ: Lawrence Erlbaum.

Pintrich, P.& Schunk. D. (2002). Motivation in education. Upper Saddle River (New Jersey): Merrill Prentice Hall.

Pittman, J. (2005). "Y'all niggaz better recognize": Hip-hops dialectical struggle for recognition In Derrick Darby and Tommie Shelby (Eds.), *Hip-hop and philosophy* (pp. 41–53). Chicago: Open Court.

Powell, M. A. (1990). *What is narrative criticism?* Minneapolis: Fortress.

Prothrow-Stith, D. (2002). Youth violence prevention in America: Lessons from 15 years of public health prevention work. In M. Tienda & W. Wilson (Eds.), *Youth in cities* (pp. 165–190). Cambridge: Cambridge University Press.

Radcliffe-Brown, A. R. (1998). On social structure. In P. Bohannan & M. Glazer (Eds.), *High points in anthropology* (pp. 294–316). New York: McGraw Hill.

Ragin, C. (1987). *The comparative method.* University of California: Berkeley Press.

Rankin, H., & Quane, J. (2002). Social context and urban adolescent outcomes: The inter-related effects of neighborhoods, families and peers on African American youth. *Social Problems 49*(1), 79–100.

Rose, T. (1994). *Black noise.* Hanover: Wesleyan University Press.

Rosenbaum, J., Fishman, N., Brett, A., & Meaden, P. (1996). Can the Kerner Commission's housing strategy improve employment, education, and social integration for low-income blacks? In J. C. Boger & J. W. Wegner (Eds.), *Race, poverty and American cities* (pp. 273–308). Chapel Hill: University of North Carolina Press.

Ryan, R. M. (1993). Agency and organization: Intrinsic motivation, autonomy and the self in psychological development. In *Developmental Perspectives on Motivation* (pp. 1–56). Lincoln: University of Nebraska Press.

Ryan, Richard, M., Sheldon, Kennon, Kasser, Tim, & Deci, Edward. (1996). All goals are not created equal: An organismic perspective on the nature of goals and their regulation. In P. M. Gollwitzer & J. A. Bargh (Eds.), *The psychology of action.* New York: Guilford.

San Antonio, D. (2004). *Adolescent lives in transition.* Albany: State University of New York Press.

Schlenker, B., & Weigold, M. (1989). Goals and the self-identification process: Constructing desired identities. In L. Pervin (Ed.), *Goal concepts and social psychology* (pp. 243–290). Mahwah, NJ: Erlbaum Assoc.

Schwartz, J. and Begley, S. (2002). The mind & the brain neuroplasticity and the power of mental force. New York: Harper.

Shaffer, D. (2000). *Social personality and development.* Belmont: Wadsworth.

Shelden, R., Tracy, S., & Brown, W. (2001). *Youth gangs in American society.* Stamford: Wadsworth.

Sheldon, K., Kasser, T., Smith, K., & Shane, T. (2002). Personal goals and psychological growth: Testing an intervention to enhance goal attainment and personality integration. *Journal of Personality, 70*(1), 1-32.

Siegel, D. (2007). The Mindful Brain. New York: W. W. Norton & Company.

Simon, H. (1994). Bottleneck of attention: Connecting thought with motivation in integrative views of motivation. Cognitive and emotion. (Ed.) William Spaulding. Nebraska Symposium on motivation. Lincoln: University of Nebraska Press.

Smedslund, J. (1984) *The invisible obvious: Culture in psychology in the 1990's.* L. Spetz & P. Niemi (Ed.S.) (pp. 443-452) Amsterdam Elsevier.

Spencer, M. B., Cunningham, M., & Swanson, D. P. (1995). Identity as coping: Adolescent African American males' academic responses to high-risk environments. In H. Harris, H. Blue, & E. Griffith (Eds.), *Racial and ethnic identity: Psychological development and creative expression* (pp. 31–52). New York: Routledge.

Spencer, M. B., Dornbusch, S. M., & Mont-Reynaud, R. (1990). Challenges in studying minority youth. In S. Feldman & G. Elliott (Eds.), *At the threshold: The developing adolescent* (pp. 123-146). Cambridge: Harvard University Press.

Stake, R. (1994). Case studies. In N. Denzin & Y. Lincoln (Eds.), *Handbook of qualitative research* (pp. 236–247). Thousand Oaks: Sage.

Stake, R. (2003). Case studies. In N. Denzin & Y. Lincoln (Eds.), *Strategies of qualitative inquiry* (pp. 134–164). Thousand Oaks: Sage.

Stipek, D. (1998). *Motivation to learn: From theory to practice.* Boston: Allyn & Bacon.

Stoesz, D. (1996). Poor policy: The legacy of the Kerner Commission for social welfare. In J. Boger & J. Wegner (Eds.), *Race poverty and American cities* (pp. 490–514). Chapel Hill: University of North Carolina Press.

Storey, J. (1998). *An introduction to cultural theory and popular culture.* Athens: University of Georgia Press.

Strong, R., Silver, H., & Robinson, A. (1998). What do students want? In A. Woolfolk (Ed.), *Readings in educational psychology* (pp. 188–192). Boston: Allyn & Bacon.

Susser, I. (2002). Information technology, The Restructuring of capital-labor relationships, and the rise of the dual city. In I. Susser (Ed.), *The Castells reader on cities and social theory* (pp. 285–313). Malden, Blackwell.

Takaki, R. (1990). *Iron cages.* New York: Oxford University Press.

Taylor, J. (2006). The mind. New York: John Wiley & Sons.

Taylor, P. (2005). Does hip-hop belong to me? The philosophy of race and culture. In D. Darby & T. Shelby (Eds.), *Hip-hop and philosophy* (pp. 79–91). Chicago: Open Court.

Thompson, S. (2005). Know what um sayin? How hip-hop lyrics mean. In D. Darby & T. Shelby (Eds.), *Hip-hop and philosophy* (pp. 119–132). Chicago: Open Court.

Tillich, Paul. (1952). *The courage to be.* New Haven: Yale University Press.

Tucker, C. M. (1999). *African American children.* Boston: Allyn & Bacon.

Urdan, T. (2001). Contextual influence motivation and performance: An examination of achievement goal structures. In F. Salili, C. Chiu, & Y. Hong (Eds.), *Student motivation: The culture and context of learning* (pp.191–200). New York: Plenum.

Urdan, T., & Maehr, M. (1995). Beyond a two goal theory of motivation and achievement: A case for social goals. *Review of Educational Research, 65*(3), 213–243.

Wade, R. (1995). The enduring ghetto: Urbanization and the color line in American history. In R. Caves (Ed.), *Exploring urban America* (pp. 72-81). Thousand Oaks: Sage.

Wartik, N. & Carlso-Finnerty, L.C. (1993). Memory and Learning. New York: Chealsea House.

Watson, J. (2006). DNA The Secret Life. New York: Alfred Knopf.

Way, N. (2004). Intimacy, desire and distrust. In N. Way & J. Chu (Eds.), *The friendship of adolescent boys* (pp. 167–96). New York: New York University Press.

Weiner, B. (1992). *Human motivation.* Newbury Park: Sage.

Weiner, B. (1998). History of motivational research in education. In A. Woolfolk (Ed.), *Readings in educational psychology* (pp. 173–182). Boston: Allyn & Bacon.

Weissman, D. (2000). *A social ontology.* New Haven: Yale University Press.

Wetherell, M. (1998). Critical social psychology. In R. Sapsford, A. Still, M. Wetherell, D. Miell, & R. Stevens, *Theory and social psychology* (pp. 5–18).Thousand Oaks: Sage.

Wexler, B. (2006). Brain and Culture. Cambridge: MIT Press.

White, J. L., & Cones, J. H., III. (1999). *Black man emerging.* New York: Rutledge.

Willis, J. (2006). Research – Based Strategies to Ignite Student Learning. Alexandria, Asco.

Wilson, A. (1990). *Black on Black violence.* New York: Afrikan World InfoSystems.

Wilson, A. (1992). *Understanding Black adolescent male violence.* New York: Afrikan World InfoSystems.

Wilson, J. (1985). The declining significance of race. In N. Yetman (Ed.), *Majority and minority: The dynamics of race and ethnicity in American life* (pp. 128-135). Boston: Allyn & Bacon.

Wilson, J. (1987). *Truly disadvantaged.* Chicago: University of Chicago Press.

Yin, R. (2003). *Case study research.* Thousand Oaks: Sage.